Fat Cat Art

Fat Cat Art

Famous Masterpieces Improved
by a Ginger Cat with Attitude

SVETLANA PETROVA AND
ZARATHUSTRA THE CAT

JEREMY P. TARCHER/PENGUIN
An imprint of Penguin Random House
New York

JEREMY P. TARCHER/PENGUIN
Penguin Random House LLC
375 Hudson Street
New York, New York 10014

Most Tarcher/Penguin books are available at special quantity discounts for bulk purchase for sales
promotions, premiums, fund-raising, and educational needs. Special books or book excerpts also can be
created to fit specific needs. For details, write: SpecialMarkets@penguinrandomhouse.com.

Library of Congress Cataloging-in-Publication Data

Petrova, Svetlana.
Fat cat art : famous masterpieces improved by a ginger cat with
attitude / Svetlana Petrova.
p.   cm
ISBN 978-0-399-17478-0
1. Painting—Humor. 2. Zarathustra (Cat) I. Title.
N6999.P485A4   2015
750.02'07—dc23   2015011539

Printed in China
9   10

BOOK DESIGN BY CLAIRE NAYLON VACCARO
AND STEPHANIE HUNTWORK

To the memory of Tatiana Arsentievna Iskuzhina,
beloved mother of Svetlana Petrova
and devoted human to Zarathustra the Cat

Circa 1955, Toksovo, Russia, self-portrait by Tatiana Iskuzhina

Contents

How I Met Zarathustra the Cat

Perhaps you were a bit surprised to see on the cover of this book that my co-author is not a human, but a Cat. It is not a joke or a marketing trick; the impact of Zarathustra on my work is so important that he fully deserves to be coauthor of our Fat Cat Art project.

First let me introduce myself. My name is Svetlana Petrova. I am a woman living in St. Petersburg, Russia. I am a graduate of the Faculty of Philosophy of St. Petersburg State University. After graduating with a first-class degree, I discovered that I am too independent to work in the "system." So I became an artist.

In fact, I had been drawing and writing poetry from childhood. My mother taught me everything, although she was not a professional artist herself. She was an engineer and a teacher of cybernetics at the St. Petersburg Naval Institute, but she was an artist in her soul. My mother made beautiful black-and-white photos, which she then painted in aquarelle colors, such as the self-portrait on the dedication page. You can see she was a beautiful and elegant woman. So it's no surprise that my path in art began in the fields of fashion and theater. I created a bizarre fashion show called L.E.M.—Laboratory of Experimental Models—and toured it all over Europe in the nineties.

I have always been very curious and liked to investigate new fields, so I decided to become an event producer. I got acquainted with lots of interesting people in my travels and wanted to present their art in my country and so I brought to Russia some live music and theater acts. Meanwhile I was interested in implanting video screens in my costumes and did so with a screen displaying interactive moving images controlled by computer. Thus I fell in love with animation. And in 2003, I created the International Festival of Animation Arts: Multivision, now one of the oldest and biggest international animation festivals, with a professional jury, in Russia. It is famous for my large-scale video installations on the raised drawbridges over the Neva River in St. Petersburg that take place each summer.

So everything was fine, and in 2008 more than fifty thousand spectators gathered at the giant video installation on the two main bridges of St. Petersburg. It was my biggest triumph. My mother was so proud of me and we spent a wonderful time in her summerhouse, once I had recovered from the hard work.

And then my mother died.

I was her only child, and other than me she just had one beloved being, a ginger Cat, Zarathustra. Of course I adopted him after her death. Zarathustra was and is a living memory of my mother. She asked me to take care of him, and so I do, as far as I can.

Here I should say that I am very close to Cats because my family always had Cats, going as far back as we can trace our history (from the nineteenth century). I grew up with a little kitten called Marussia, or just Murka, who was the same age as me. I would say we developed some kind of telepathic liaison. It was so sad that she died from old age when I was only fifteen! So it is natural for me to understand Cats.

Then our family had an unbelievable ginger Cat called Vladimir Vorotnikov, or simply Vova. He was a philosopher and a talking Cat. You know Cats try to imitate human speech when you talk to them often. It's a known fact that was revealed by a group of zoological psychologists. Other zoological psychologists who differ on this point, by the way, are not worthy of their degrees!

As well as Vova, I had an adorable Cat-actor named Marcus Aurelius Wolfgang Amadeus. Marc the Cat performed in my shows *Swan Lake II* and *Moulin Russe* . . . wherein he played the role of the God of Mice, wearing wings made of feathers that perfectly matched in color his gray tabby fur.

Marc the Cat performing in L.E.M. theater

After my mother's death, I sank into the most terrible depression. I was so close to my mother. I missed her so much, and I am still missing her.

And it was Zarathustra who saved me from that depression.

One day a friend said to me: "You created such amazing art with your Cat Marc in your L.E.M. shows. Why don't you do something with your new Cat, Zarathustra. He is so funny!" And he was: he was fat; my mother spoiled him immensely. As my mother herself would say, he is "the best Cat in the world."

I thought: "Why not? It will distract me from my grief," and I began to think what I would do. It was useless to put wings on him like on Marc, because Zarathustra is clearly unable to fly, with his physical condition. So I thought that maybe I could make a photo session with food in the style of Dutch still-life paintings. To imagine how it would look, I decided to photoshop Zarathustra into such a painting. I had used Photoshop for sketches of the sets for my events and costumes. And I don't know why, but I photoshopped him into another painting, *Danae* by Rembrandt. Then I did this with four more classical paintings and sent them to some friends, who are artists and collectors, just to see their reaction.

Never before have I seen serious ladies weeping, and having to lie down, from laughing. I received so much praise: "How naturally Zarathustra fits into the paintings!," "It reveals something new in their meaning," something that made people happy.

The impression was so good not just because my artistic skills had been validated but because of the work of Zarathustra. In fact, he is a natural-born artist and he knows he is making art. Zarathustra adores posing when people are taking photos of him. He is always very friendly to photographers. He knows who is a photographer and begins to flatter those people. It's amazing how he knows!

He has found a special place for work as a model. In my apartment there is a podium covered by a big carpet—it looks like a stage. When Zarathustra wants to pose, he shows me that I should go there, then he lies down on this carpet and begins to make very funny poses with a very serious face. He has a rich repertoire of mimicry and can make different expressive grimaces. The camera likes him.

Despite having this star character, he is a very sensitive and tender Cat, a real gentleman, or better, a "gentlecat." Everybody who meets him is astonished and says that he is somebody special. He really is ten kilograms (twenty-two pounds) of pure undisturbed joy.

Concerning his weight, it may sound strange, but he eats very little. Actually, he is trying to lose weight by keeping to a very strict diet of high-quality veterinary Cat food. If on occasion he wants something tastier, he chooses only healthy treats, such as raw beef and king prawns. King prawns are his favorite food, but of course not more than three prawns per week.

My heart bleeds forcing him to be on this diet, but what can I do? However, I can say that he tolerates the diet restriction with dignity, much more dignity than I would have being on a diet.

The very positive reaction to my first experiments with Zarathustra encouraged me a lot, and I launched the site FatCatArt.com in February 2011. I put it online and then left it. I wanted to see if it would spread naturally, without any effort from my side. At that time I was occupied with other projects.

In late autumn, at the closing event of my animated film festival Multivision, one of the film directors noticed Zarathustra's image in my portfolio and asked me why I had this image. I answered, ". . . because I made it," to which he responded, "Why don't you have a look at the Internet? It's full of your Cat!" I explored the Internet and was astonished: Zarathustra was everywhere.

In fact, I was always interested in Internet culture. I dreamed of making an experiment: to create an Internet meme that would be both beautiful and clever. I liked this idea both practically and philosophically. This virus should bring some information, create some stimulus to know more. It should be a virus of freedom for aspiring to new knowledge and not a virus of simply repeating what has been done before.

People who discover my Cat paintings are likely to google for the originals. Of course not all of them do that, but just a few of them doing so makes it worthwhile. The "Cat-infused" paintings fit perfectly with my idea of a clever and beautiful meme.

Making this project has brought me a lot of knowledge also. I have studied in detail the style of the old masters, their technique. Now I can make my paintings look as if they are real paintings made by an old master, in spite of the fact I have inserted a photo of a modern kitty, using a computer.

I should say that digital media gives people incredible possibilities to interact with art. If you change something in the digital image, it doesn't change anything in the real world.

In the real world, changes can be destructive, but in the world of information, changes can lead to its growth. You can destroy the physical support to information, but you cannot destroy information itself; it's nonmaterial. With digital media, art became not something untouchable: now we can touch, we can communicate with it.

I want people to be more curious, to aspire to new knowledge and skills. I think everybody can be creative, and I think my art stimulates them to be.

Everybody should have the right to be an artist, even a Cat!

Though the digital part of the Fat Cat Art project is important, it is not the only one that makes an artistic impression. In fact, it is a sophisticated mixture of photography, painting, and performance that is put together by the computer and me. I call this new technique "digital integration."

The working process is as follows:

1 I have an idea to make a new work: I have an inspiration from thinking about life around me, or from an existing work of art, or from what Zarathustra is doing in his life.

2 I get the images of artworks in high resolution.

3 I take the Cat's photos. I make photos of Zarathustra when he wants to pose, and he really adores posing. He insists that I take photos, and he is upset if I have no time to do this! I also have special photo sessions with him, where I am helped by my friends—professionals in the art sphere. We amuse ourselves a lot doing this.

4 Then I carefully photoshop the Cat into the right position in the painting's digital image. It is the lengthiest and most difficult part of the work; he must fit ideally, in position, in expression, and sometimes it takes months to take the right photo. And there must be no trace of the previous person.

5 Sometimes I do a lot of work on the rest of the picture, emulating the style of the great master. The Cat image, which is a digital modern photo, should also be in the style of the older painting. At the same time it must stay an Internet "cute kitteh."

6 Then comes the text commentary: I compose that also. The Cat speaks in a special language and in a special style. I just imagine what Zarathustra could tell about this or that fact in our life if he could speak. Or he is just telling me something without words, as all Cats loved by humans do. Don't think that I'm crazy saying this; all of us can find the ring of King Solomon on one's finger if one has enough desire, attention, patience, and love for animals.

The Cat blog is bilingual, Russian and English, and I was helped in the creation of English CatSpeak by Anthea Norman-Taylor, who had the idea of curating and hosting the exhibition in England, *From Icons to Icats*, in May–June 2014. This exhibition showed that Fat Cat Art is a serious art project and not just an Internet meme.

For exhibitions, my digital pieces are printed on natural canvas as used for paintings. Then I finish them manually with a brush, applying texture gels and oil colors, including very rare historical pigments made from precious stones such as lapis lazuli (which, for example, is a very important color in Vermeer's *Milkmaid*). Thus our images look like real historical paintings, even in texture and color, and it seems that a master of the past painted a Cat in it.

Anthea even had trouble at customs in the St. Petersburg airport with one of these digital paintings. It was Venetsianov's *Spring*. The customs officer thought it was an old painting, a national treasure that you cannot export. My friend tried to explain: "Do you think an old master would really draw giant Cats in place of horses?" She had to scratch it with her nail to show it had a printed base!

MEWSINGS

And this complicated multilayer project turns around a simple domestic Cat! One could say, "Indeed, that is so." Cats have become quite important in modern human culture. Why are Cats so popular on the Internet? This question has become as important as the question about the origin of the Universe. I have also thought a lot about it.

I think that the Cat is the totem animal of modern city tribes and the Mews (Muse) of contemporary Internet art and megapolis folklore and mythology.

They worshipped Cats in Egypt, the native country of mathematics; so do people of the modern digital era. The omnipresent and omnipotent Kitteh rules on the Internet. The Cat's independence and self-esteem are highly appreciated by the anonymous user, the main inhabitant of the World Wide Web. It possesses the amazing ability to get into where nobody else can get and to do whatever it wants. For this the street artist also gives so much value to Cats. For metropolis inhabitants, petting a Cat is the only chance to enjoy nature. Cat as a trickster makes urban bustle and Internet traffic a game, causing CATHartic laughter of people exhausted by civilization.

Do you remember the déjà vu scene in the movie *The Matrix*? The multiple Cat appearance signals a glitch in the matrix, so an abundance of Cats on the Internet signals that our human life should be changed; humans should walk by themselves and think by themselves, as Cats do. Maybe that is why kitty's image has become so popular among modern humans.

The Cat image language is a universal one. People understand its meaning without words, so this language unites nations.

And this is indeed something mysterious: that in this strange period of human life I met this extremely talented Cat—Zarathustra.

In his personality digital interpretations of old masters' paintings, contemporary appropriation art performance, and Internet Cat meme came together.

FOR THE ART HISTORIAN AND ART CRITIC

According to the term that was invented by French art historian Agathe Lichtensztejn, the genre of our work is "ready-meme." It's a ready-made 2.0 . . . a ready-made of the digital era.

She writes:

The strength of Svetlana Petrova's statement is similar to Marcel Duchamp's ready-made *L.H.O.O.Q.* . . . We define ready-memes as such: they are works built in the continuity of Duchamp's gesture, hosting the encounter between two distinct cultural paradigms. It is formed by a picture of a sovereign masterpiece of art, facing an Internet meme, which idea originally comes from collective online production. Because the ready-meme is a work of art, he tells us from where he comes. The artist and the manufacturing process are determined. Because the ready-meme is a meme, it does not tell us where he is going. It is the work developing by contagion, and virality continues the history of art forwards.

During my childhood my mother and I went to the Hermitage Museum every weekend.

Then Zarathustra the Cat came into my life, and it was like he was sent by my mother to take care of me in her absence, and to bring me again to the art museum.

Now I pass you to his soft paws so that he will do the same for you: he will guide you through the history of art and the world's most famous museums.

St. Petersburg, Russia
October 2014

Fat Cat Art

Thus Speaks Zarathustra the Cat

"OUR LIFE AS MEWS TO THE GREAT ARTISTS WE ADMIRE"
BY ZARATHUSTRA THE CAT

Our name is Zarathustra. We are a Cat. According to our assistant (named by ignoramuses as Our "owner"), We are the best Cat in the world. We are also very, very fond of Arrt. Much of Our postprandial time is given to reflection upon lofty matters. We are also quite gracious in Our enjoyment of repasts.

Our main passion, however, is to sit for the great artists. Only great artists can appreciate Our generous body and sublime soul.

Through the centuries We have graced many of history's greatest artistic masterpieces, walking by Ourselves from painting to painting, revealing to humans what is real Beauty. We should tell Our story from the very beginning. . . .

Rembrandt Harmenszoon van Rijn, *Danae*.
Thus the great Rembrandt depicted Our noble postprandial reflections.

23

PART I

Ancient World and Middle Ages

Fat Horse and Fat Cat

Everybody knows that the first famous painting in the history of humanity is a horse painting from Lascaux Caves.

But have you ever noticed that the horse is actually FAT?

Yes, in noble ancient times (long before the dawn of today's glossy magazines, which celebrate all these poor starving creatures), the word "fat" implied not "over-fed" but "powerful," "wealthy," and "happy."

Here We are the Fat Cat and the Fat Horse, models on the red carpet, going to the first ever vernissage at the cave.

It was the beginning of Our journey through the History of Arrt, which We will now introduce to you, moving from one century to another.

Lascaux Cave wall painting, Fat Horse and Fat Cat

Walk Like an Egyptian, but Hunt Like an Egyptian Cat

An amazing discovery was recently made by British scientists: using X-rays, they discovered a mysterious ancient Egyptian Cat fresco hidden beneath the famous wall painting at the Tomb of Nebamun that now resides in the British Museum.

The central spot in the masterpiece is reserved for Us, Zarathustra the Cat. We are so kind to accompany a human, an Egyptian official, Nebamun, during his hunt in the marsh, generously pointing out to him what We'd like to have for Our dinner. Meanwhile an Egyptian girl gives to Us a tender belly rub using a lotus, while another girl waves a fan to save Us from overheating. A typical ancient Egyptian scene, you know.

They say ancient Egyptians trained wild Cats to help them hunt, though nowadays people assume only dogs can play the role of helper (by the way, some Cats can also play fetch).

If you look at the fresco that covers the hidden one, currently on view in the British Museum, you will notice a less Cat-centered Universe.

It's evident that mankind underestimates how much ancient Egyptians really worshipped Cats!

P.S. The Internet is a lot like ancient Egypt; people write on "walls" expressing their worship of Cats.

Please, humans, don't just write on walls. Take the time to *actually* worship your Cats, please. Right now, please go and give a good belly rub to your kitty.

Hunting in the marshes, Tomb of Nebamun, Thebes, around 1350 BC

Plato's Symposium

This fresco of a symposium in the time of Plato was found on the north wall of the Tomb of the Diver, in Paestum. Our companion (second from the left) entertains himself with Kottabos, a noble game that involves flinging what is left in a glass of wine at a target. Some ignoramuses might recklessly suppose that We are the target. . . .

Symposiums were way more entertaining in Plato's time than nowadays, weren't they?

Symposium, Paestum, Tomb of the Diver, 470 BC

The Battle Cat

We were immensely kind to play the role of Bucephalus sitting for Roman mosaicists at the House of the Faun in Pompeii. The mosaic shows Alexander the Great fighting in the Battle of Issus. As Roman mosaicists well knew: with the help of your Cat you will win the world.

Alexander the Great riding the Fat Cat at the Battle of Issus, Pompeii, 100 BC

The Bayeux Tapestry—
The Mystery of the Twenty-Third
Scene Revealed!

After the happy and fun ancient Greek and Roman times came the mysterious Middle Ages.

There is a common belief that this period of time was not favorable to Cats because they were required to serve as companions to the devil. It is not true! According to recent investigations, the Spanish Inquisition is in fact an invention of the early Renaissance (and Monty Python, of course).

Cats were also worshipped during the Middle Ages, but in an esoteric way. Medieval people loved secrets, you know.

The Bayeux Tapestry, true twenty-third scene, 1070

Here, We are going to reveal one of these hidden moments from the cult of Cats of the time—the mystery behind the twenty-third scene of the Bayeux Tapestry—a very popular medieval comic strip embroidered on a 70-meter-long (230-foot-long) linen canvas. The scene depicts an event that finally led to the Norman invasion of England.

The captions read: HAROLD SACRAMENTUM FECIT WILLELMO DUCI—"Harold made an oath to Duke William."

But what oath? Nobody actually knows! The only thing that is clear: Harold didn't fulfill his promise, and the result was more than sad for him.

Here We show what really happened there—and what was embroidered initially on the canvas:

Harold brought to Duke William an armchair that his beloved Cat found unbearably small.

That is why everybody is evidently upset at the scene, discussing what to do and why Harold was so stupid to buy such a tiny chair for such a large Cat.

After examining his mistake, Harold exclaimed to William: "I swear I will provide a bigger chair for your Cat!"

But he did not.

The rest you already know: Halley's Comet was seen in the sky. The Normans invaded England. William became the Conqueror.

Don't Beware of the Apocalyptic Cat!

Do you remember an angel with many eyes in his wings in the movie *Hellboy* by Guillermo del Toro and the seven-eyed goat in *Altered States* by Ken Russell?

Do you know that this innovative way to observe unusual and complicated situations with more than two eyes was invented not by modern cinema directors but by the twelfth-century masters of Romanesque art in Catalonia, Spain, who depicted Apocalyptic animals that were "full of eyes"?

Here We are, Apocalyptic Cat seen with Apocalyptic Lamb on the apse of Sant Climent de Taüll, the Church of St. Clement of Tahull. Our restoration works reveal the Cat taking part in this important event of human history. Stay near to Us Cats during the Apocalypse: We are as full of misericordia as We are of eyes. Just find your place in between the Lamb and Us.

Thus speaks Zarathustra the Cat.

Note: The Lamb and eye-winged seraphim are actually to be seen at MNAC, the national art museum of Catalonia in Barcelona. And now, dear Catalonian government, can you please award Us with a domain .cat site address for this amazing discovery?

Apocalyptic Lamb and Apocalyptic Cat from the Church of Sant Climent de Taüll, 1123

Gentile da Fabriano, *The Adoration of the Cat*, 1423

The Adoration of the Cat

We, Zarathustra the Cat, now point your attention to a popular subject of many famous medieval paintings: the Adoration of the Magi. Have you ever wondered why one can always find a lot of animals in the paintings—there are cows, donkeys, and even dogs—but you never see a Cat there! This is because the many (yes, there are many) paintings of this sort that featured Us were pilfered. In order to correct this historical injustice, We present to you one such painting, *The Adoration of the Cat* by Gentile da Fabriano. Note that babies have adored cute Cats from time immemorial. And in turn, We try to stifle the urge to swipe at them with our paws—even when they do the unthinkable and grab our tails in their moist little palms.

The medieval page in human history closed with the International Gothic style as depicted in this work. For Us Cats it meant that humanity was about to step into the glorious Renaissance era, which revived the ancient cult of beauty. Which meant, of course, that the worship of Cats was about to receive a much-needed breath of fresh air. . . .

PART II

Italian Renaissance

The Man and the Cat

While today Man and Cat portraits quite literally litter the Internet (have you had a look at Tumblr lately?!), such images were rare during the Italian Renaissance. Rare but not *that* rare.

Here, We, Zarathustra the Cat, reveal a second diptych of Urbino that has heretofore been hidden from public view: portraits of the Duke of Urbino and his Cat by Piero della Francesca. We present the first Renaissance painting in which a Cat worshipper "came out."

Just compare this masterpiece to the famous first Urbino diptych by Piero della Francesca, to be found in the Uffizi Gallery in Florence. These facing portraits of Federico da Montefeltro and his wife, Battista Sforza, were commissioned by Montefeltro after his beloved wife's passing. What is far less known is that after Battista passed away, Federico found consolation in the care of her beloved Cat. Looking at the Cat, he saw his wife. Though he couldn't speak to her, he could speak to the Cat, hug the Cat, and love the Cat. We Cats are mystic entities that can walk between worlds, connecting humans that are separated by time and space. It was this ability of Ours that Piero della Francesca depicted in his second Urbino: portraits of the Duke of Urbino and his Cat.

We remember that sitting! We were so tired to sit for the artist in a jeweled collar and a diadem. The portraits were hidden because people were saying: "Crazy Cat guy alert! Federico gives too much importance to this Cat." It was a cruel time in which people thought it was somehow unserious for a man to love Cats. Dogs and horses, OK, as they served in hunting and battle, but not Cats. Now that humans are feeling less afraid to share their love for Cats, the time has come to reveal this second Urbino diptych.

Feeding Your Winged Cat

Perhaps you have seen Paolo Uccello's famous 1470 painting *Saint George and the Dragon*? If so, it will interest you to know that this is not the original painting. The original painting featured Us and it had a hidden agenda. Uccello was a fervent Cat lover and wanted to remind humans that an important part of Cat worship is feeding your Cat in a correct and healthy way.

Uccello advised to feed your winged Cat with fresh raw meat.

A dialogue:

"My kitty is so fat, he gained so much weight that he cannot fly anymore, poor thing!"

"Madam, you should feed him only organic food, often but in very small portions!"

Paolo Uccello, *Saint George Feeds the Winged Cat with Organic Food*

Venus Heavenly and Earthly

Here is the true look of *The Birth of Venus* by Sandro Botticelli.

The idea behind this far superior original depiction of a Heavenly Venus (as opposed to the commonly known version that is most unfortunately celebrated) was developed by Botticelli in partnership with his friend and Plato disciple Marsilio Ficino, who noticed that We graciously love repasts and symposiums.

And, by the will of the gods, We love all other things, only in a platonic way. . . .

Sandro Botticelli, *The Birth of Venus*

The Secret of Mona Lisa's Smile Revealed!

Mona Lisa's smile is a mystery no more. She smiled because We were there. In fact, We challenge anyone with twenty-plus pounds of immeasurable grandeur on their lap to stifle a smile!

In response to the critics and gallerists of his time who viewed any pictures with Cats in them as unserious (why, We know not), Leonardo reluctantly painted out Our image. And yet Mona Lisa's smile remained. This is the true story.

Leonardo da Vinci, *Mona Lisa*, true version

Cats and Glamour

Some say that Cats are not glamorous beings, as evidenced by the fact that today's fashion-addicted young ladies prefer to carry handbags, tiny dogs, or tiny dogs in handbags, for that matter!, to other accessories. Back in the Italian Renaissance fashionable young ladies such as Cecilia Gallerani, the subject of Leonardo da Vinci's famous painting *The Lady with an Ermine*, found ermines to be just the thing to carry as an accessory. Or did she? You may have wondered why such a stylish young femme would want to be seen with a suspiciously mouse-like little creature such as this. In point of fact, she did not. Have a look at the original version of the portrait of Cecilia Gallerani.

It might interest you to know that on the day of the sitting, We enjoyed a sumptuous dinner with the lady herself at Duke Sforza's palace at which it was discussed how truly luxurious Our coat is in contrast to that of the ermine. We also learned how very happy the lady was to serve as Our accessory in this portrait of Us.

Some ignoramus (likely a dim-witted gallerist who thought that he could fetch a higher price for the piece if it featured a higher-priced chunk of fur) had the painting altered. Be that as it may, We feel vindicated that the world now recognizes that Cats are the most elegant beings on Earth.

Leonardo da Vinci, *Lady with a Cat Pretending to Be an Ermine*

LA BELE FERONIERE
LEONARD D'AWINCI
FATCATART

Happily Ever After

Today We, Zarathustra the Cat, reveal to the world the true look of *Venus of Urbino* by Titian.

If you have a look at the commonly known version of the masterpiece in the Uffizi Gallery, you will notice that Venus of Urbino looks a bit . . . bare. And the expression on her face is one of longing. This is because the beautiful lady in the sketch (as opposed to her counterpart in the true version of this painting) was left only dreaming of a handsome, warm, and soft Cat! Yes, the commonly known version was just a sketch, and the purrfect final version was hidden by Illuminati as precious secret knowledge. Now We reveal it.

Cats can warm you on cold winter evenings. They also can hide all that is not for children's eyes ☺☺☺. Note how content Venus is in this true version of the masterpiece.

Titian, *Venus of Urbino*

The Organ of Venus

We cannot only lie beside Venus, but lie instead of her, so lovely are We. Great Titian thought so when he painted us as the glorious subject of the organist's gaze (is it Us or is he focusing in a most odd way on Our lower right nipple?). And what is it that Cupid is whispering in Our ear? We'll never tell. . . .

Venus's Selfie

Titian is famous for his portraits of Venus. One of them, *Venus with a Mirror*, has the nickname "Venus in furs." No, it is not because of what you are thinking.

It is because human memory still keeps in its subconscious the true look of Titian's *Venus*.

Left: Titian, *Venus with the Organist and Cupid*

Right: Titian, *Venus with a Mirror* or *Venus in Furs*, true version

How to Worship the Golden Cat
by the Whole Nation

Filippino Lippi and his followers (it's usual to say disciples) created an epic canvas showing an outstanding example of Cat Worship in the ancient world. What a joyful view, to watch from above a crowd of minions praising Our felinity!

Filippino Lippi, *The Worship of the Golden Cat*

The Creation of cAt-dam

Here We, Zarathustra the Cat, reveal to the world the original version of the famous Michelangelo fresco that *should* (if there were any justice in the world) be on view in the Sistine Chapel today: *The Creation of cAt-dam*.

A bit of background: In the Hebrew language "ādām" means "human" and is linked to its triliteral root אדם (A-D-M), meaning "red," "fair," "handsome." OMG, why can't you humans see it! It's so evident! Adam was a ginger Cat!

Michelangelo, *The Creation of cAt-dam*

Raphael, *Cats Are the True Angels* (fragment of *Sistine Madonna*)

Cats Are the True Angels

The winged cherubs on the bottom edge of the *Sistine Madonna* by Raphael are, of course, mega-famous. In the last two centuries they have had an extraordinary career in advertising and mass culture, making appearances on stamps, postcards, calendars, and T-shirts. In fact, name the tchotchke and they've been there and done it. The story goes that Raphael was inspired by two kids he encountered on the street, who were staring wistfully into the window of a food shop. They looked so serious, as if they were contemplating the meaning of life. The artist thought to himself that they would make for a very nice detail in a painting he was working on. The true story is that there was actually just one kid. And by his side? We, of course.

A footnote: It was, in fact, the deep intelligence, which marks beings who are searching for the true meaning of life or a shank of smoked ham, displayed on Our face, that was the stronger influence on Raphael's decision to feature the boy and Us in his great masterpiece.

Appreciating the whole composition, one can see that now it is easy to understand what Saint Barbara is actually looking at.

Ah, see how much more moving the original version of Raphael's painting was? Of course, art critics of the day forced the great master to paint over the Cat—street children are more or less OK, but not Cats! Yes, sadly, We must say it again: We were not seen as "serious."

Right this moment please go and kiss your Cat on its nose because your Cat is a true angel.

Gentlemen Prefer Cats

As the legendary home of all art, Parnassus was rather a popular subject in Renaissance painting. In his original depiction of the magical mountain, Andrea Mantegna revealed the mysterious connection between Cats and Arrt, showing how crucial felines are to the artistic process.

Andrea Mantegna, *Parnassus*

Now look closely: Mars is hugging Cat Venus.

Vulcan is teasing Cat Anteros, representing heavenly love as opposed to carnal love.

Apollo is playing his lyre to a Mews.

Mercury is speaking to Cat Pegasus.

What an idyll!

Girls—Muses—seem to be slightly jealous. Maybe they would like to have just a little bit of carnal love? No way in the presence of heavenly love!

Music of Heaven

Do you know the true music of heaven?

It is the mewsic of kittens saved from the streets or bad people!

P.S. Please donate money to the nearest Cat shelter so the mewsic of heaven will continue to play through eternity.

Rosso Fiorentino, *Musical Angel-Cat*

FATCATART

Respect

In rare moments of Arrt history we see past and future collide.

As a case in point, here is the original version of one of the paintings in Paolo Veronese's famous series entitled *The Four Allegories of Love*. It's called *Respect*. That's right, Respect as in R-E-S-P-E-C-T.

In the painting you see Snoop Lion (a timeless icon if there ever was one of Respect as in R-E-S-P-E-C-T), whose appearance on the hip-hop stage Veronese foresaw in this picture from 1575. Then you see a very respectable classic Cat and, finally, a naked sleeping lady. Everybody is stylish and has Respect for each other.

Perhaps you would like to know why one cannot find this beguiling version of the painting at Britain's National Gallery and can instead see only a later remake? This is because when Veronese presented the original version of the painting in 1575, the art establishment guys told the artist: "A cute Cat in an official painting? Respect for a naked babe? An African man? Hasta la vista, baby!"

"I beg your pardon. I'll fix it immediately," whispered Veronese, trembling. You know what time it was. Now, finally, We restore the truth.

And now We shall move from sunny Italy to the north to see what happened during the Renaissance there.

Paolo Veronese, *R-E-S-P-E-C-T to Cats and Lions, Featuring Snoop Lion*

Wine vs. Catnip

If you are a human of some Cat, you may notice that your master is not very happy if you occasionally drink a glass of good (in your opinion) wine. We Cats find alcohol shocking in its smell. Of course, We can just kindly tolerate human assistants when they entertain themselves with it.

So can you imagine what a challenge it was for Us to sit for Caravaggio while he painted his famous *Bacchus*!

We played the role of a panther, Bacchus's mascot.

We were so disturbed by the glass of wine in the hand of a human model pretending to be an ancient Greek god of alcoholic drinks.

Only a few leaves of catnip in Our paw saved Our tender nose from this madness. We feel so sorry for Bacchus's panthers. What a hell of a job they got!

After the session only three drops of heavenly valerian could save Us from sad thoughts about their destiny!

Caravaggio, *Bacchus*

PART III

Northern European Renaissance and the Sixteenth Century

The Familiar Stranger

O f all Our experiences sitting for great artists, this was one of the weirdest. One day in 1834, in the great city of Bruges, the great master Jan van Eyck invited Us to be his Mews. We should sit for him. We found Ourselves in the company of the familiar stranger.

We quickly discovered that this man was very fond of expensive clothes and jewelry. He put a golden chain on Our neck and a fur-decorated mantle on Our back. The green color of the clothes harmonized perfectly with Our natural coat, a fact that diverted Our attention from the sadness of thinking about how many animals died for lining the mantle. (We hope they were mice, which We eat and from whom We are struggling to defend the museums.)

The man raised his right hand in the gesture of an oath and gave Us his left hand. Proffering his left hand meant at that time that he didn't consider Us an equal person; men often think that Cats are inferior to them. Showing all Our goodwill, We gave him both Our soft honest paws. By the end of the sitting, he was putty in Our hands. Still, art critics at the time were unhappy. They wanted a woman in place of a Cat. Yes, dear readers, it was another regretful decision on the part of an artist that led to the version of this masterpiece now on public view. It is Our hope that someday the true version will take its place.

Jan van Eyck, *The Arnolfini Portrait,*
The Man and the Cat

Hieronymus Bosch,
The Catwain

The Catwain

ere We present the true version of the central panel of *The Haywain Triptych* by the great Hieronymus Bosch. This true version is entitled *The Catwain*. Five centuries ago, in his geniusness Bosch predicted the dawn of kitty celebrity as we know it today. It is a marvelous time indeed when Grumpy Cat earns more than Robert Downey Jr. Of course Bosch thought better of revealing his prophecy to his contemporaries, who would likely have put him in a madhouse. Still, the artist felt the desire to realize his vision through his art and so he asked Us to sit for him. After satisfying this need, he later painted a warm, sweet, pleasantly scented stack of fresh hay over Us. It was cozy for Us and made the paintings palatable to his contemporaries.

We do admire the original painting in which a famous Internet kitty is being transported to some sort of vanity fair. We are so gloriously large, a wagon is needed to bear Us. To where do you think we are being transported? . . . Maybe to some vanity of celebrity like *Good Morning America* . . . or even *The Oprah Winfrey Show*.

The wagon is accompanied by a crowd of ignoramuses engaged in a variety of sins—some of them are making hate comments on YouTube, some just disturb the kitty's privacy, trying to tickle him by all manner of means, and some even seek to profit from his popularity. The Cat is definitely confused, though he doesn't forget to try to steal a fishy from a non-attentive person; obviously this crowd completely forgot his food delivery schedule!

A group of ignoramuses make fun of the large Cat's back. Near them, an angel exclaims, "OMG!" His exclamation is addressed to Christ, looking down on the scene from the sky. His eyes are full of sorrow. He knows well how popularity can be dangerous for an innocent being!

Can Cats Be Friends with Birds and Rodents?

It has been said, quite unfairly, I might add, that Cats have a hard time sharing a home with other animals. That We chase and paw at birds and squirrels and the like. This is not so! Especially if We live in the house of a serious animal lover such as the lady depicted by Hans Holbein the Younger in the painting now popularly known as *A Lady with a Squirrel and a Starling*. With such a one as she, We can share a home with other animals quite peacefully! Note how Our gracious self was actually included in the original version of the painting. See how affectionately the lady holds Us in her arms (We are, after all, a good deal cuter than any bird or squirrel).

Hans Holbein the Younger, *A Lady with a Squirrel, a Starling, and a Cat*

Venus and the Cat Hunting Birds

They say that We Cats are natural born killers. But don't forget that humans introduced Cats to their society precisely *because* of Our hunting abilities. Now humans take the mission of rat genocide upon themselves, by means of chemical weapons that are much more cruel than Our noble hunting. And still humans complain about Our cruelty! What hypocrisy!

In the commonly known version of this painting in the National Gallery of Denmark in Copenhagen titled *Venus with Cupid Stealing Honey* by Lucas Cranach the Elder that exists today sans Us, Cupid complains to his mother, Venus, that the bees sting him because he has stolen their hive. Venus replies that his love arrows also hurt.

At the top of the original painting one can find a quotation from the previously unknown version of a fable by the ancient Greek poet Theocritus.

We dared to translate it from Latin as such:

Dum cattus venantur aves in horto
domina quoque cauda captat
Sic etiam nobis brevis, et peritura voluptas,
Quam petimus, tristi mixta dolore nocet.

While boyish Cat hunted birds in the garden,
his human caught him by the tail.
Thus, too, the brief and passing pleasure that we seek,
ends in Obesity Management diet.

Because of you, dear humans, We Cats abstain from hunting pleasures and instead humbly munch dry food. You should have more respect!

DOMINA QVOQVE CAVDA CAPTAT
SIC ETIAM NOBIS BREVIS ET PERITVRA VOLVPTAS
QVAM PETIAVS TRISTI MIXTA DOLORE NOCET

FATCATART

Lucas Cranach the
Elder, *Venus with the
Cat Hunting Birds*

Your Feline Savior

Do you remember the first sequence of Lars von Trier's *Melancholia*? What happened in this moment in the film is quite similar to the scene depicted in Lucas Cranach the Elder's enigmatic masterpiece. That true version We now present to you.

Who is the stylish winged lady in this painting? Why is she definitely not happy watching the children play? She looks anxious. What is going on?

Our restoration to the original helps to resolve this question.

Now we see a common city scene: three brothers are playing with the Cat, and doing so without any respect, as children often do.

The Cat, according to the tradition of Our noble race, humbly lets little humans do with Him whatever they want, even things for which an adult being would be punished without mercy.

Their mother is anxious: "Children, please, don't torture our kitty! Leave him alone, he wants to sleep!"

Nobody in this peaceful scene notices the signs of something really bad about to happen, symbolized by the drunks (or maybe junkies?) riding past on pigs in the left corner of the painting.

Don't worry, the Cats are here to save you! Look closely and you will see the following:

In the distance a Cat avatar watches from afar.

He is literally sitting on a volcano, generously sharing his large body to keep it from erupting.

Sitting on the window ledge another Cat avatar guards the scene. His determination to maintain peace by all means is emphasized by the strong gesture with which he steps on a bird's tail, demonstrating that nobody, even this small creature, will disturb the happy family.

Remember, with a Cat (or two) in your home, you will be safe!

Lucas Cranach the Elder, *Melancholia of City Cats*

Cats That Fixed the Tower of Babel

We, Zarathustra the Cat, now present the original version of Pieter Bruegel the Elder's most famous painting, which appears to have been a diptych. Here is the first part of it. Further details follow, and the second part after.

The commonly known version of this painting is the pearl of the Museum Boijmans Van Beuningen collection in Rotterdam.

We, the time-traveling Fat Cat, visited the painter when he began to work on the story of the Tower of Babel. Having cuddled and tickled and snuggled a lot his visitor, Bruegel thought that the epic failure of humanity would never happen if there would be enough Cats among humans: everybody would sink into cuteness and stop quarreling and Cat lover's language would become universal. And he started to paint.

Pieter Bruegel the Elder, *The Tower of Babel*, diptych, part 1

Cats see deep into the future . . .

and watch small people under their paws . . .

And kindly show themselves through a window to an excited audience . . .

finish the construction playing . . .

relax on the balcony . . .

In order to help humans, Cats throw things from the top . . .

they sleep in unexpected places . . .

and hunt you from unexpected places.

But having seen the original painting, art critics of the sixteenth century told Bruegel: "Come on, Pieter, it looks like you installed a Cat Paint app on your iPhone! It is not serious enough! Don't be a boy, you are the Elder! And moreover, it is blasphemy!"

Against the advice of his heart, Pieter Bruegel painted over the Cats.

But in the silence of his atelier he painted another version of the tower, a blueprint for future generations showing how to repair it and to unite the nations again.

Pieter Bruegel the Elder, *The Tower of Babel*, diptych, part 2

Now both parts of the Rotterdam diptych are united with the commonly known version in the Museum Boijmans Van Beuningen.

Don't believe this photo? Just go and check the Museum Boijmans Van Beuningen!

Dolce Far Niente

Every Cat is a top professional when it comes to laziness, and We, the best Cat in the world, are a true champion of it.

After all this work on fixing *The Tower of Babel* made with Pieter Bruegel the Elder, We really needed a good rest after a good and tasty dinner, of course.

While We were enjoying our postprandial time, the great master painted Us once again. He imagined a fabulous land where food has legs and arrives to a hungry stranger saying to him: "Eat me!" The only effort you would make in this land is chewing your food and stretching after a good nap.

Pieter Bruegel the Elder, *The Land of Cockaigne*

Fat Kitchen

itchen dramas were important even in the sixteenth century, and it was Pieter Aertsen who profoundly investigated the impact of food on human history's most basic moments.

Here we can see the profound reflection on how Cats, being carnivores, can yet live with vegetarian humans.

Vegetarians don't want to eat meat, Cats don't want cabbage: that is the drama of *The Fat Kitchen. An Allegory* by Pieter Aertsen.

The question remains open for centuries, as some humans don't stop in their efforts to turn Cats into vegans.

Please don't!

We Cats are unable to digest food made only from plants. Morality exists only when you have a choice. We Cats don't ask you to breathe in water like fish do, as you have no choice in this question. We realize that thus you will die and then will not provide Us the food that We deserve.

So please be realistic also.

Now please go and give a nice piece of food to your Cat companion.

Pieter Aertsen, *Fat Kitchen. An Allegory*

Phœnix

Aquila

VERBO DOMINI FIRMATI SUNT COELI, ET SPIRITU ORIS EJUS OMNIS EXERCITUS EORUM, Psalm. 33. SPIRITUS DOMINI REPLEVIT ORBEM TERRARUM : OMNIA SATIANTUR BONITATE TUA DOMINE : AVERTENTE TE FACIEM, TURBANTUR : AUFFERS SPIRITUM EORUM, ET DEFICIUNT ET IN PULVEREM SUUM REVERTUNTUR : EMITTIS SPIRITUM TUUM ET CREANTUR : SIC RENOVAS FACIEM TERRÆ : GLORIA TUA IN SECULUM. Psalm. 104.

RUFUS HERMETIS TABULA.

Verum, sine mendacio, Certum & verissimum: Quod est inferius, est sicut quod est Superius, & quod est Superius est sicut quod est inferius ad perpetranda miracula Rei Unius. Et sicut omnes Res fuerunt ab Uno, meditatione Unius: Sic omnes Res natæ fuerunt ab hac Una Re Adaptatione. Pater Ejus est Sol, Mater Ejus Luna. Portavit illud Ventus in Ventre suo. Nutrix ejus Terra est. Pater omnis Telesmi totius mundi est hic. Vis ejus integra est, si versa fuerit in terram. Separabis Terram ab Igne, subtile à spisso, suaviter cum magno ingenio. Ascendit à Terra in Cœlum, iterumque descendit in Terram, Et recipit Vim Superiorum & Inferiorum. Sic habes Gloriam totius Mundi. Ideò fugiet à te omnis obscuritas. Hic est totius fortitudinis fortitudo fortis, quia vincet omnem rem subtilem, omnemque solidam penetrabit: SIC MUNDUS CREATUS EST. Hinc erunt Adaptationes mirabiles, quarum modus hic est. Itaque vocatus sum Hermes Trismegistus, habens Tres partes Philosophiæ totius Mundi. Completum est quod dixi de Operatione Solis.

Ginger Sun

When it is cold, humans have a unique chance to heat themselves: their ginger suns, their golden Cats.

Wise Hermes Trismegistus, author of *The Emerald Tablet*, also known as *Tabula Smaragdina*, which contains the secret of the *prima materia* and its transmutation, knew this. This lost secret knowledge shows that *The Emerald Tablet* was written for a bright green summer; for the pale winter, Hermes Trismegistus created another sacred text, *Tabula Rufus*, aka *The Ginger Tablet*.

Here is the text of *The Ginger Tablet*, translated by Isaac Newton and found among his alchemical papers just recently. It differs much from the commonly known text of Sir Isaac's translation of *The Emerald Tablet*.

Matthäus Merian der Ältere, *Tabula Rufus. Macrocat and Microcosm.*
Etching from the book *Basilica Philosophica*, 1618

The wisdom of *prima materia* is the Cat and its transmutation:

'Tis true without lying, certain & most true.

The Cat which is below is like the Cat which is above & the Cat which is above is like the Cat which is below,

to perform miracles of only one thing

And as all things have been & arose from the postprandial meditation of one Cat: so all things have their birth from this one Cat by adaptation to his needs.

The Sun is the Cat's father, the moon the Cat's mother, the wind hath carried it in its belly, the Earth, and above all living on it, the Cat's human is its nurse.

The father of all perfection in the whole world is here kitty, kitty.

The Cat's force is entire if it be converted into Earth to dominate it.

Separate thou the earth from the fire, the subtle from the gross, sweetly and with great industry prepare thou tasty meals for your Cat.

The Cat ascends from the earth to the heaven & again it descends to the earth & receives the force of things superior & inferior when you play with your Cat using a laser pointer.

By combing the Cat you shall have the glory of the whole world

& thereby all obscurity shall fly from you.

The Cat's force is above all force. For it vanquishes every immaterial thing & penetrates every solid thing if the Cat wants something.

So was the world created.

From this are & do come admirable adaptations, i.e., pots, bowls, combs, laser pointers whereof the means (or process) is here in this. Hence I am called Hermes Trismegist, giving three parts to the philosophy of the whole world.

That which I have said of the operation of your Ginger Sun is accomplished & ended.

You can check the text of *The Emerald Tablet* and agree with Us that *The Ginger Tablet* is way wiser.

Take care of your ginger sun and the Cat will make your days warm and cozy.

PART IV

Dutch Art in the Seventeenth Century

The Cat's Concert

What can be more refreshing for our human friends than Our loud meooooows at the crack of dawn?

The great Dutch painter Frans Snyders knew this and depicted an outstanding cultural event in his masterpiece.

The not yet purrfect sketch to this original version of the painting that rests in the Hermitage Museum of course has no . . . wait for it . . . Cats. It's just a bunch of birds chirping away in the later version entitled *Concert of Birds*. The Dutch proverb that follows sums up the problem with this version succinctly: "Elck vogeltge singt soo't gebeckt is"—"Every bird sings the way he knows how," meaning "Everyone speaks the way he knows how." And We know how to speak!

Frans Snyders, *The Cat's Concert*

The Cat's Introduction

You've adopted a Cat from a shelter. You are living with your parents and brothers and sisters and don't know how to introduce to them a new member of the family?

Here is depicted some advice from the seventeenth century: host an official gathering to introduce Us.

Bartholomeus van der Helst, *Family Portrait*

Finding Our Milky Way

This nice and warm Friday evening We chose for comfort the Milky Way.

If you compare this true version of Vermeer's masterpiece with the version exhibited at the Rijksmuseum in Amsterdam, you will see that this first one makes more sense.

Without a Cat, the kind woman is sad: she has nobody to care for, nobody to serve this nice fresh milk!

A nice reminder that when you drink warm milk on a calm Friday night, please don't forget about your Cat!

Johannes Vermeer, *The Milkmaid and the Cat*

Fat Boy and Fat Cat

Did anybody mock you because of your weight in your childhood? Maybe somebody called you "Fatso" or "Big-Bellied Ben"? Don't be upset, these people don't understand true and purrfect Beauty.

Let us have a look at this famous portrait of the young Gerard Andriesz Bicker by Bartholomeus van der Helst, which often serves as an example of how spoiled the seventeenth-century Dutch aristocracy was, perhaps because of Gerard's chic costume, the smug look in his eyes, and of course his general plumpness. As if personal fat storage has some correlation to personal wealth. Nonsense! The original version of the masterpiece reveals a very different scenario.

We see Us, Zarathustra the Cat, appearing from the folds of Gerard's silk outfit.

Maybe Bicker was not so fat after all? This boy at the young age of seventeen already held many responsible offices and had a lot of other things to do than just enjoy his meals.

Maybe the reason for his big belly was simply that he loved his fat Cat so much that he brought him everywhere, hidden in his rich costume. The warm and furry Cat napping at his belly may well have helped him to resolve difficult human problems. We all know how allowing a Cat to sleep on your belly can instantly remove the weight of the world! The portrait suggests that when Gerard was called such things as "bacon burger," he would put his hands on his napping Cat and say firmly, "Go

Bartholomeus van der Helst,
Fat Boy and Fat Cat

away, you idlers." But at that moment the Cat appeared from his costume folds and said, "Wait a minute, Gerard, a BURGER—is what that We just heard?"

Peace and friendship were instilled immediately, and the boys all together hurried to feed the Fat Cat.

Aelbert Cuyp, *Peasants with Four Cows and One Cat by the River Merwede*

Cat and Cows

Aelbert Cuyp, the famous Dutch landscape painter, loved to decorate his panoramas with large animals: cows and horses and the like.

Yet once he met Us, he immediately fell in love and gave Us as much space in his landscape as he felt We deserved.

Jan Steen,
The Merry Family

The Merry Family

Remember: the way to happiness in every house is to have a Cat in it!

Soap Bubbles and the Cat

How transitory life is! How quickly it passes by! We have just finished Our dinner, and We are hungry again. . . . This feeling of the brevity of Our existence is strengthened by the severe diet that We have chosen in order to obtain health and make Our life longer. What an irony of fortune!

Yes, Our dinner was like soap bubbles: we barely bite down, and nothing is left . . .

Thus spake today We, Zarathustra the Cat, after eating dietary crisps for a snack.

You will find more reflections on the transitoriness of dinners and life in general in the famous still life paintings of the Dutch golden age in the following pages.

Karel Dujardin, *Boy Blowing Soap Bubbles and Cat Hunting for Them.*
Allegory on the Transitoriness and the Brevity of Life

PART V

Dutch Still Life in the Seventeenth Century

The Cat Chef Recommends

For a good breakfast the Cat chef recommends crab! With this wise advice We, Zarathustra the Cat, begin the section of Our book dedicated to the Arrt of Still Life and to the Arrt of Cooking. Or as French people say in a very catlike manner, *la naturrre morrrt et les gourrrmiaoundises.*

Who can imagine the art of still life without the Dutch old masters and their discreet yet charming bourgeois breakfasts?

But you should notice how this still life and those that follow in the coming pages become real life when a Cat is added to the painting! Cats improve everything, but Cats are really best at improving still lifes.

As a matter of fact, most everything that you usually see in a still life painting was prepared for a Cat or at least repurposed by a Cat for their own pleasure (hey, if you leave it on the table, We see it as fair game!).

Take a look at the not-yet-finished version of this painting that hangs on a wall in the Hermitage Museum. You can see how lonely the crab appears without a Cat to take care of it!

Willem Claesz Heda, *Cat's Breakfast with a Crab*

Adriaen van Utrecht, *Still Life Improved by Cat*, 1644

And Where Is the Russian Salad?

Dutch still life of the golden seventeenth century is a realm of opulence where one can find everything one wants. But it works so much better if you add a Cat to it.

Look how the Cat's noble presence ameliorates the colors of the gifts of Nature, because He Himself is the best gift ever! If you don't believe Us, just compare this Cat-infused still life with the inferior version at the Rijksmuseum in Amsterdam.

Now We ask Ourselves if one can find really everything in the opulence of Dutch still life.

Well . . . no, because where is this famous Russian salad, called in its homeland Salad Olivier? It is the most traditional food for every family party. We are so gracious in Our enjoyment of repasts that We demand that every opulence should be included in our still life!

We must add the Russian Salad Olivier! Here is a heavenly recipe for this most heavenly of salads composed by Our humble assistant's grandmother, who was famous for her dinners. The recipe has some essential secrets.

INGREDIENTS:

7–10 ounces bologna sausage (better from beef and pork). Other meats can be used instead: baked beef, boiled chicken, but Doctorskaya sausage is the most authentic. It is similar to bologna and is made with beef and pork. In the United States, look for "baby sausage."

3–4 medium potatoes (Secret!: Never use more than 4 potatoes!)

2 large carrots

2 hard-boiled eggs

3–4 Russian salted cucumbers, or maybe more, depending on the size of the cucumbers (in some places they call them dill pickles, to be found in Russian, Polish, and Jewish food shops)

1 large Granny Smith apple (Secret!: A Fuji apple is also OK.)

1 bunch fresh dill

1 can (15 ounces) green peas

½ cup mayonnaise mixed with ½ cup sour cream or plain yogurt, or ⅔ cup mayonnaise mixed with ⅓ cup sour cream or plain yogurt, depending on your taste (Secret! This mixture gives your salad a heavenly taste and aroma.)

Horseradish sauce to taste

METHOD:

1. First and most important: Serve a slice of bologna to your Cat. If the Cat approves your choice of sausage, that is, kindly eats it even if he is not hungry, you may proceed. If he does not approve it, please find another sausage. So, your sausage is happily approved.

2. Boil the potatoes and carrots until cooked. Put them in cold water until they are cool and ready to peel. Peel the potatoes and carrots.

3. Place the eggs in a small saucepan and cover with cold water. Bring the water to a boil over high heat, then reduce the heat to a simmer. Cook the eggs for about 20 minutes, then put them in cold water. Peel them when they have cooled down.

4. Dice the bologna, potatoes, carrots, eggs, pickles, and apple. All diced items must be the same size as a pea. (Secret!: Only the apple can be diced a little larger because when you bite into them you feel satori.) (Secret!: The pickle cubes can be smaller because they play the role of salt. Never put salt in your salad; you should just add more finely chopped pickles if it is not salty enough.)

5. Chop the fresh dill.

6. Put all the diced ingredients together in a large bowl and add the dill and the peas. Then add the mayonnaise–sour cream mixture. (It is better to begin with a proportion of ⅔ cup mayonnaise to ⅓ cup sour cream; then you can add sour cream to taste.)

7. Mix everything thoroughly. (Secret!: Add a little bit of horseradish sauce.)

Our assistant's grandmother put this chef d'oeuvre into a cut-glass bowl and decorated the top of the salad with fresh dill and an artificial mushroom made of a hard-boiled egg and half a red tomato with little spots of white mayonnaise. And all human children dreamed of getting this beautiful mushroom, though it was definitely not the tastiest part of the famous salad!

Be so gracious in your enjoyment of repasts!

How to Measure a Lobster?

Today We, Zarathustra the Cat, can give an answer to a question that has tortured humanity for centuries: what size lobsters are the most tasty?

This is the right size.

While looking at this masterpiece of the Dutch genius of still life at the National Gallery in London, one can easily see that this delicious lobster needs to be measured. And it should be measured by a professional, which means by a Cat. A nice dark space is reserved for this measurer in the painting.

It is another brilliant demonstration of Our theory that Dutch still life is created for Cats.

Sirs and Mesdames, don't forget to get your lobsters measured by a Cat!

If you don't have lobsters, you can give your prawns to your Cat for measuring.

Willem Claesz Heda, *Still Life with a Lobster Measured by a Cat*

Pieter Claesz / Питер Клас
Vanitas / Суета сует
1625

s a n e

i n s a n e

True / Правильно

Bezrukov / Спасибо, что живой

n e u t r a l

f * c k i n g   i n s a n e

False / Не правильно

Kanye West / Спасибо, что в очках

Pieter Claesz, *Vanitas for Dummies*

Vanitas, the Cat, Kant, and Kanye

Vanity of vanities; all is vanity. All . . . brands, cars, diamonds, and Kanye West. To begin with, Pieter Claesz drew the Cat meditating on his expectation of the inevitable dinner.

Then, being scared by a well-known art critic's reaction, he painted a human skull over the Cat. Thus human civilization was stopped in its development, and the result is sadly well-known.

Humans often prefer to think about the things the existence of which outside Us should have to be assumed merely on faith, as genial German philosopher Immanuel Kant would say. Of course he meant diamonds, huge cars, branded clothes, and other big boys' and girls' gadgets.

But a noble one should be satisfied with the preprandial transcendental unity of apperception. In this sophisticated term Kant meant that the Cat's dinner exists because he has its idea in his mind, and existence of other things is more than doubtful for the noble being.

Kids, read Kant from early years and have your own happiness.

The Cat and the CATalogue

They say that Cats are very egocentric beings and thus they are subject to vanity. This is far from the truth: it is not vanity; it is purely justified self-esteem. And of course We Cats like it when others value us correctly.

We, Zarathustra the Cat, were pleased to be asked to create this book that is in fact a CATalogue of Our noble mission to improve famous paintings. The famous master of *Vanitas Still Life*, the Dutch painter Edwaert (or Edward in English manner) Collier created a masterpiece to commemorate this notable event.

One can find the commonly known version of this painting in the Rijksmuseum and understand Our wise idea that every still life painting aims to be visited by a Cat!

This famous master also created a self-portrait depicting himself working on this painting.

If you compare this version with the commonly known version at the National Portrait Gallery in London, you will notice that in Our version, the sense of what is happening becomes clearer.

Edwaert Collier, *Vanitas: The Cat and the CATalogue*

Some ignoramuses think that We are just a LOLcat. They don't notice Our subtle perfection—what a shame!

And We would like to ask these people: have your ever heard about Edwaert Collier before visiting this page? Have you ever seen the commonly known versions of ALL the paintings in this book? We bet no.

That is why We have one other reason for Vanitas: Our Cat's noble educational mission to improve mankind.

Edwaert Collier, *Self-portrait with Vanitas: The Cat and the CATalogue*

PART VI

Flemish Art in the Seventeenth Century

Three Graces

O ne day We so graciously visited the great Flemish artist Peter Paul Rubens that he decided to commemorate this visit with a painting.

The story of its creation is very dramatic.

Peter Paul adored Our generous grace and wondered for a long time which Grace we should represent, Aglaea or Euphrosyne? (We are too gracious for Thalia.)

He came to the right solution: the more Cats the better.

Peter Paul Rubens, *Three Graces*

The Judgment of Paris

Rubens painted Us in his other famous painting where he reflects on the question: what is Beauty?

He reveals the true appearance of Helen of Troy, to whom the prince Paris chose to give an apple, judging her the most beautiful being on Earth.

No doubt about it: Helen of Troy was a fat ginger Cat!

Peter Paul Rubens, *The Judgment of Paris*

Abduction of the Fat Cat

Some Cats are so beautiful that humans have upon occasion had severe disputes as to who might be so honored as to give a home to such a breathtaking feline.

Rubens depicted such a situation in his famous painting.

Two guys just grabbed an extremely beautiful fat ginger Cat from the backyard of the daughter of Leucippus's house. The girl noticed them and ran to save her kitty in such a hurry that she had no time to put her clothes on.

Caught at the crime scene, the guys suggested to the girl: "Maybe you also will come to live in our place with this Cat?"

"No way!" the girl shouted. "I don't need you! Just give me my Cat back!"

Peter Paul Rubens, *The Abduction of the Fat Cat from the Daughter of Leucippus*

Your Personal Bacchus

Created in the last years of Rubens's life, the *Bacchus* painting amazes the spectator with its unusual interpretation of the image of the god of wine and merriment. Bacchus is depicted as a grossly obese Cat, surrounded by a satyr, a maenad, and chubby kids. According to Rubens's nephew, Philip, this was not a commissioned work, and the artist kept it in his studio till the end of his life. The painting was inherited by his nephew after the death of the artist. Poor guy, being afraid of all well-known art critics' reactions, he asked some disciple of Rubens to paint a man over the Cat. That version of the painting can be seen at the Hermitage Museum.

Peter Paul Rubens, *Bacchus*

Twenty-Two Pounds of Pure Undisturbed Joy

Have you ever tried to take a walk with twenty-two pounds of Cat? Anthony van Dyck once tried, and this experiment inspired him to create this painting.

Anthony van Dyck, *Drunken Silenus Supported by Satyrs, or Strolling with a Fat Cat*

Fat Cat Party

A nice Flemish tradition to make parties for their Cats became the subject of David Teniers the Younger's painting.

Just now, please, go and make a party for your Cat!

We are now done with Flemish art and will move on to Spanish art in the seventeenth and eighteenth centuries.

David Teniers the Younger, *Twelfth Night. The King Drinks*

PART VII

Spanish Art in the Seventeenth and Eighteenth Centuries

Hugging Your Cat with Your Left Hand

Why do people refer to that "crazy Cat lady" and never a "crazy Cat gentleman"?

Men like Cats no less than women do, as we know by Our website visitor statistics.

The genius El Greco painted one of these devoted male Cat lovers.

El Greco, *The Nobleman with His Cat on His Chest*

Riding on Your Cat

We adore the Prado Museum collection. To celebrate this feeling of true love We kindly gave Our back to Philip IV of Spain.

N.B.!: Please don't try to ride a Cat in real life unless your Cat is as big or bigger than a tiger or a lion. On second thought, even in this case We strongly recommend you don't to try to ride on his back.

Diego Velázquez, *Philip IV on Catback*

Playing with Your Cat

We proudly present the recently found original version of the world-famous painting by the great Spanish artist Francisco de Goya, a kind of sketch commissioned by the royal tapestry factory for a series of tapestries to be hung in the office of King Carlos IV at El Escorial.

Though this work made him famous, Goya was not happy painting it. He thought he could be creating far more important work (all artists felt the same throughout the centuries!). After the tapestries were produced, this painting, along with the other sketches, were forgotten for centuries, only to be discovered in 1860. They were restored and donated to the Prado Museum.

Goya created the first version of the cartoon in 1791, centuries after the end of the Spanish Inquisition, but the political climate in the country was still far from joyous and free. In the original sketch Goya painted four girls enjoying their game with the big orange Cat.

Unfortunately the client, the Royal Tapestry Committee, didn't approve the design, so the artist created another, bigger version (now in the Prado), where he painted the sad straw mannequin instead of the joyful Cat. We happen to know that with the straw doll Goya was depicting himself as he felt his will had been so stifled by a patron that would not allow him the freedom of artistic expression in the form of a big orange Cat. By the will of the gods, this original sketch with the Cat was recently found. We are willing to kindly donate it to the Prado Museum. We want people to discover it and to realize that an artist must feel himself like a joyful Cat, and not as a mannequin dependent on the dictate of clients, the will of politicians, the caprice of fashions, tendencies of the market, or the taste of art critics. Only then will Beauty save the world.

Francisco de Goya, *Forget the Straw Mannequin or Have More Fun with the Cat*

Venus in Furs

In 1651 Diego Velázquez finished his famous *Venus at Her Mirror*. Most of the world is familiar with his Venus's delightful back. But nobody knows its true version.

At the time every Spanish artist was afraid of the possibility of another Spanish Inquisition's unexpected return. (You should watch Monty Python's reenactment of what this historic happening might have looked like to understand how terrifying it might have been had it actually transpired.) As during the Inquisition, police severely punished the drawing of any naked body, so artists were still fearful.

Well, this particular Spanish genius found a solution: he painted a naked Cat. Velázquez knew that not only would this keep him safe from persecution, but a Cat makes everything better.

Some years later fear of another Inquisition had faded and Velázquez was pressured to insert the typical naked lady into his painting in place of a big orange Cat. We are deeply saddened by this decision as *Venus in Furs* with actual fur is clearly so much more sumptuous to behold than naked human skin. Ah well.

Diego Velázquez, *Venus at Her Mirror*

PART VIII

British Art in the Seventeenth and Eighteenth Centuries

Cat Ladies

Here We present a pleasant example of Cat ladies in early seventeenth-century Britain.

According to an inscription in gold letters in the bottom left of the painting, the portrait shows "Two Ladies of the Cholmondeley Family, who were born the same day, married the same day, and adopted Cats from a shelter on the same day."

What noble behavior!

British School, seventeenth century, *Cholmondeley Cat Ladies*

Not Gonna Get Us

And now We shall visit a most notable British masterpiece by Sir Henry Raeburn in which he portrays Reverend Robert Walker enjoying a favorite winter sport.

Here, on a frozen Scottish lake, far away from the fireworks of political controversy, the message the painting sends is clearly "not gonna get us." Politics are completely absent from the scene. Only sport is present here. Sport and, of course, excellent company.

Let Us compare Our version to the commonly known one that may be contemplated at the Scottish National Gallery. It is evident how much the minister in the true version of this painting far prefers to not skate alone as he thinks upon lofty matters—that he far prefers the silent company of the Cat.

Sir Henry Raeburn, *Reverend Robert Walker Skating on Duddingston Loch,* aka *Skating Minister and Skating Cat. Not Gonna Get Us!*

How Was the Universe Created?

I n this work William Blake answers this important question.

William Blake, *The Ancient of Days*

Surprised Kitty

Do you know how to play "surprised kitty"?

It's not very difficult. You can find an OK Go tutorial for it online. But beware of playing it with the Great Red Dragon. He will always cheat!

William Blake, *The Great Red Dragon and the Cat Clothed with the Sun*

Beware of the Laser Cat

If somebody is cheating in the "surprised kitty" game, Our tolerance ends very soon.

Better not to do this, because everybody knows that the main weapon of the Internet kitty is not claws, but lasers!

William Blake, *The Great Red Dragon and the Great Laser Cat*

PART IX

French Art in the Eighteenth and Early Nineteenth Centuries

A Ginger Cat and a Red Hat

D o you know that French clergyman, nobleman, and statesman Cardinal Richelieu was a devoted Cat lover? In 1642 he had fourteen felines! But here's a fact We are confident nobody knows. On one occasion the cardinal had the pleasure of meeting Us. And so greatly did he enjoy Our company that he gave us his red cardinal's hat!

Philippe de Champaigne, *Portrait of Cardinal de Richelieu*

The Cat's Kiss

According to the myth of eternal return, We, Zarathustra the Cat, were so kind as to return every six o'clock in the morning in order to kiss a certain young female.

Only initiated people know how refreshing a Cat's kisses are in the early morning.

Jean-Honoré Fragonard, *The Stolen Kiss*

Two Pusses with Two Odalisques

O ne day We graciously met up with a couple of charming ladies in the Palais du Louvre and kindly sat with them for one of the greatest French artists of all time.

We became the second Grand Odalisque for Ingres.

Jean-Auguste-Dominique Ingres, *Deux Grandes Odalisques*

Jacques-Louis David, *Le Chat avec Madame Récamier*

And We graciously spread out on Madame Récamier's sofa in just the same pose that We use to lie down on Our favorite armchair.

Cats Rule the World!

You know that Napoleon suffered from a complex about his short stature? That is why all his portraits flatter him immensely. Really, how did he actually look? He was very small in height compared to other humans. In fact, he was as small in comparison as We are to humans, a fact that was not lost on the painter of this famous piece by Jacques-Louis David.

Napoleon loses his famous triangular hat in the rush. The genius brushstrokes of the great master vividly depict this epic moment in human history.

Unfortunately Napoleon wanted an official portrait, and David flattered his client a lot in his five other well-known versions of this masterpiece. One can find one of them in le château de Versailles. Another is to be seen in le Louvre.

But We know that only a Cat deserves to be Emperor of the Universe (or, if this position doesn't yet exist, maybe for now a president or a prime minister—just suggest something).

Jacques-Louis David, *Napoleon Crossing the Alps*

FATCATART
BONAPARTE

Cats Are the Emperors of the Universe

Even if Napoleon was not actually a Cat, he was definitely enamored with Us. This fact about the great dictator—that he had a very particular weakness for Cats—is here depicted by Jean-Auguste-Dominique Ingres, who showed Us sitting on Napoleon I as if the emperor himself were just an Imperial Throne for the Cat.

Just compare this masterpiece to the commonly known version of the painting that one can see at the Musée de l'Armée, Hôtel National des Invalides in Paris.

Please answer for yourselves the following question: which version is more true to life?

Of course Ours!

Cats are the true Emperors of the Universe!

Jean-Auguste-Dominique Ingres, *Napoleon Used as Imperial Throne for the Cat*

The True Pussy Riot

Did you know that the true pussy riot is not a Russian punk band? The term was originally used to describe a time at the end of winter when Cats who have not been relieved of their animal desires (or "neutered," as humans often refer to it) search for love and understanding in very unusual and inappropriate places. As they make their merry way, they sing, dance, and, on occasion, get into fights. Most of the time all of this festivity does not bother humans, but We do understand that the heavenly harmony of Cats' voices on a peaceful and still night might disturb other creatures' meditations. Still, We value all creatures' (and most of all Our) right to the pursuit of freedom, health, and happiness and so it was that the great Eugène Delacroix originally selected Us to represent the concept of Liberty in his famous painting. See how lovely We look dancing on the barricades in this picture. In Our noble embrace of nonviolent protest, We throw away the gun and dance with the banner, hoping to make people laugh out loud and thereby stop killing one another.

Sadly, when the painting was complete, males who were not relieved of their animal desires asked for a topless girl and a lot of blood.

Oh those humans!

Eugène Delacroix, *Liberty Leading the People,* or *The True Pussy Riot*

They are so addicted to shock-horror news as delivered by the press as they eat their breakfast that they cannot be satisfied by a peaceful resolution of the conflict! We were quite disappointed that Delacroix succumbed to their pleas to insert a topless girl in our place.

Don't worry. We Cats are working on your, humans', consciousness in order to cure this addiction. Cats are unique beings on Earth; Cats can be famous without insulting or injuring anybody. It is so easy to provoke hatred among humans with different views. It is much more difficult to cause laughter and love, such as we, famous Internet Cats, do.

A special word of advice on the pussy riots of today. We use the term to denote those situations on the Internet where some humans begin to quarrel about politics or all-too-human matters. A true pussy riot is when, in response, one simply posts a cute kitty photo. If it doesn't work, you do it again. Finally, any group of quarreling humans, no matter how blood hungry, will sink into Our cuteness and begin to feel sorry for themselves for all their hate speeches.

And true pussy riots work. We have tested this method.

By the way, one can see the widely known version of this masterpiece in the Palais du Louvre, where a French king and queen lived before they were beheaded, according to the animal desires of some humans.

PART X

American Art in the Nineteenth Century

The Original Declaration
of Independence Revealed!

What a breathtaking discovery! My dear friends, We are happy to reveal to the world the original version of John Trumbull's *Declaration of Independence*. This lost masterpiece was discovered by the gracious efforts of Ourself and Our beloved brother Hank the Cat, who ran for Senate in 2012 and collected seven thousand human votes and $16,000 toward Cats' charities.

The painting depicts the moment on June 28, 1776, when the first draft of the Declaration of Independence was presented to the Second Continental Congress.

Less than a week later, on July 4, 1776, the colonial delegates signed the Declaration, a milestone in American history. As with all art, there is much symbolism to be found here. We are holding the hand of John Adams, who wrote in regards to the Trumbull painting: "Do not let our posterity be deluded with fictions under the guise of poetical or graphical license." Adams was concerned that this fictitious portrayal of history would lead Americans to believe this is how history happened—and, of course, one of his concerns was the lack of Cats in the painting.

John Trumbull, *Declaration of Independence*

Thomas Jefferson gently strokes Hank's ear—both are Virginian and both believe deeply in their country. Charles Thomson is seen tugging gently at Hank's leg, trying to pull Hank into the fighting political arena. Benjamin Franklin is seen behind Hank, with a similar pose to Zarathustra's—this represents how in early post-perestroika Russia, many people would hold on to their "franklins" (American hundred-dollar bills) to have a stable currency in order to purchase goods. Finally, Hank is seen lying on the Declaration papers—as all Cats know, the more important the papers, the better to lie on.

The commonly known version of the painting can be found at the Capitol Rotunda. The story of the versions is as follows: This is the first completed painting of four Revolutionary-era scenes that the US Congress commissioned from John Trumbull in 1817 and purchased in 1819.

Trumbull was fully content with his work, but the congressmen were not. Time went on, and history turned into mythology, so they thought that Trumbull had some fantasies about the presence of Cats on the scene. He really did have some fantasies, depicting people who were not there and not showing others who were present; this is true. But this was not the case with the two Cats. Just imagine how any household could be managed without Cats at that time? Who would struggle with rats and guard the food for humans?

But what to do? Finally Trumbull obeyed the clients (sadly the destiny of many artists) and created the version without Cats.

But Cats were on Capitol Hill in the past! And they should be there in the future! Our beloved brother Hank the Cat would have been a senator, if only his life had not been so short!

Dedicated to the sweet memory of Hank the Cat.

An Unexpected Journey

Here is the true version of the famous painting by Emanuel Leutze.

The painter invited Us to pose for this painting because he cared about the people in the boat: "It was so unbearably cold there, they needed a large warm Cat beside them to heat themselves!"

Emanuel Leutze, *Washington Crossing the Delaware in a Boat Piloted by the Fat Cat*

Whistler's Mother and the Cat

Speaking about American art, we decided to reveal to the public the original version of the most famous of Whistler's paintings.

Whistler originally envisioned painting the model standing up, but his mother was too uncomfortable to pose standing for an extended period, so she sat down. At that moment We climbed onto her lap.

The work was prepared for the 104th Exhibition of the Royal Academy of Art in London, held in 1872. One academician saw the painting in the artist's atelier before the opening and advised the Academy to exclude the Cat from the painting. He thought that the exhibition curators would not see the subject of the painting—"a granny with a Cat"—as appropriate for their very serious event. Whistler obeyed the advice, and of course the painting came within a hairsbreadth of rejection by the Academy. This episode worsened the rift between Whistler and the British art world; this was the last painting he submitted for the Academy's approval.

One can find the "official" version of the painting at the Musée d'Orsay in Paris.

James Abbott McNeill Whistler. *Arrangement in Gray, Black, and Ginger No. 1. Whistler's Mother with the Cat*

Madame X and Monsieur Z

Not only did We, Zarathustra the Cat, pose for the great American painters with old ladies. We also posed with stylish young ladies, all of whom admired Our beauty so much that they frequently chose Us as companions for their portraits.

Here is Sargent's masterpiece, depicting two extremely elegant beings.

You can visit Madame X alone at the Metropolitan Museum of Art in New York. But don't forget to ask the nearest guide, "Please show me the version with the Cat."

John Singer Sargent, *Madame X and Monsieur Z*

PART XI

Russian Art in the Eighteenth and Nineteenth Centuries

An Unknown Woman and a Well-Known Cat

Not only elegant beauties in America loved to be portrayed with Us; Russian ladies did as well!

Evidently this very fashionably clothed young woman loved her Cat so much that she embroidered the vet collar of her feline friend in the style of her gorgeous hat! This glorious collar not only cured the Cat's body, but also the Cat's soul.

You should compare this true version of the masterpiece to the commonly known version to be seen at the Tretyakov Gallery in Moscow.

We dedicate Our discovery to all veterinary doctors of the world, and especially to Our friends from St. Petersburg!

Ivan Argunov, *Portrait of an Unknown Woman in Russian Costume and a Well-Known Cat in a Vet Collar*

The Cat as the Symbol of Justice

The great Russian empress Catherine II chose Us to represent Justice on her official portrait made by famous Russian painter Dmitry Levitsky.

"Everything for the sake of the Cat!"—that is what her broad gesture tells the spectator.

"Please give Us this everything immediately, and please give Us more of it!" says Our broad gesture in reply to the empress.

Dmitry Levitsky, *Portrait of Catherine II with Cat as the Symbol of Justice*

A Cat Rider

W e also once kindly lent Our back to a young lady who was posing for Karl Bryullov, a famous Russian painter with Italian roots.

A nearby dog could not even bark from astonishment at Our generosity.

Karl Bryullov, *The Cat Rider*

What If Leo Tolstoy Wrote His
WAR AND PEACE on Tumblr?

We decided to reveal a version of Tolstoy's famous portrait by Ilya Repin. We can compare this version with the commonly known one, to be found at the Russian Museum in St. Petersburg.

There you will not find this theme of the relationship between creator and public, which We brought to the famous painting.

Would you say that it's impossible that such a serious writer could play silly kitty Cat games on a social network?

Of course he could do this. Don't forget that his name, Leo, means "lion," and that means "a Cat," a great Cat, but still a Cat!

What is also important in this Tumblr version of the famous painting is the good belly rub given to Us by the great writer.

A good belly rub is one of the most precious things in the whole universe! Just trust Us.

Ilya Repin, *Leo Tolstoy with the Cat-Beard, Barefoot*

The Cat in Winter

Russia is as famous for its snowy winters as it is for its literature.

By the will of the gods, wrapped up in Our cozy abode We are relieved not to feel the outside chill that pervades during this time of the year, but Our heart is still full of mercy for the creatures in this original version of Vasily Perov's masterpiece.

Vasily Perov, *Troika. Apprentices Fetch Water with the Kind Help of Cat*

Fatcatart

207

Jingle Bells

Sometimes strange events happened in Russian history during the wintertime.

Vasily Surikov, *Boyarynya Morozova*

Spring Is Coming and Coming!

It was the time when peasants in Russian villages began to prepare their big ginger Cats for plowing their immense fields.

Alexey Venetsianov, *In the Plowed Field. Spring*

The Ninth Life

We look terrible but are full of mercy.

Due to the figure of a caring Cat, the sea appears to be not so menacing and gives hope to the people. He will give one of his nine lives to save them.

Ivan Aivazovsky, *The Ninth Wave, or Ninth Life*

Russian Cats or Russian Bears?

We and Shishkin know the right answer.

The truth is that Konstantin Savitsky had painted the Cats but the art collector Pavel Tretyakov effaced his signature, stating that "from idea until performance, everything discloses the painting manner and creative method peculiar to Shishkin," so the painting is now credited solely to Shishkin, and there are bears instead of Cats.

To be seen at the Tretyakov Gallery in Moscow.

Ivan Shishkin, *Morning in a Pine Forest*

Unequal Marriage

Mostly We serve as a model for beautiful characters or heroes.
But once We were invited by the great Russian painter Vasily Pukirev to play the role of an elder who marries a young girl against her will.

Unequal marriage means that the woman is sold to her husband, although she hates the man.

But now We, the Cat, play his role. Maybe the girl will be happy? She will turn her head and notice that there is a young, energetic, and beautifully fat Cat, instead of an old man to whom it would be so boring to give a good belly rub!

Vasily Pukirev, *Unequal Marriage*

The Hunters at Rest

Who wants to listen to the Cat's hunting stories?
   ". . . and it was this big! . . . and We jumped and grrrrrh! Rwawww!"
   "Oh, really? You are just kidding!"
You know, human hunters do just the same.

Vasily Perov, *The Hunters at Rest*

The Russian Hero Cat

Everybody knows about Our extraordinary heroism. For example, I'm sure you've heard of Tara the Hero Cat.

Russians especially appreciated Our fighting abilities. Russian knights never went to battle dragons without a Cat.

Viktor Vasnetsov, *Russian Heroes (Bogatyri) and the Russian Hero Cat*

The Cat in the Underwater Kingdom

The centerpiece of Our famous exhibition *From Icons to Icats*, which was held in the UK in 2014, was a masterpiece by Ilya Repin, *Sadko in the Underwater Kingdom*. The painting features a story from a Russian folktale. Sadko the merchant arrives in the Underwater Kingdom and sees a parade of beautiful submarine princesses, but he thinks about his fiancée in his homeland.

During restoration works, it appeared that the master had painted an underwater Fat Cat as the symbol of wealth that seduces the merchant.

Ilya Repin, *Sadko and the Underwater Fat Cat*

His fiancée, who is seen to have rescued a stray kitty, symbolizes the appeal to charity that every merchant should follow for the sake of humans and Cats in need.

This painting, alongside eleven others that We feature in and We present in the Russian art sections of this book, was exhibited in a beautiful seventeenth-century former granary barn.

Generations of Cats hunted mice there, generously helping humans to keep their harvests safe. Now We came to the barn also to help humans, to make them recognize Internet memes as a new genre of art.

PART XII

Japanese Art in the Nineteenth Century

Happy End of the World Day! (Part 2)

We Fat Cats can feel Ourselves in complete comfort even in the conditions of a tsunami. So We Cats shall take care of you, humans, don't worry.

How uncomfortable the end of the world in general and the condition of a tsunami in particular would be to humans who try to survive without Us, the Cats! One can see the commonly known version of Hokusai's work at the generous site of the Library of Congress.

Katsushika Hokusai, *Great Wave Off Kanagawa or Happy End of the World Day!*

OS CISNES VOAN DO ALTO DO CEU
JOVENS MULHERES QUEREM EM UM BAR
OLHOS VERMELHOS

ЛЕБЕДИ ЛЕТЯТ ВЫСОКО В НЕБЕ
ДЕВУШКИ ХОТЯТ В БАР
КРАСНЫЕ ГЛАЗА

白鳥は、空高く飛ぶ
女の子はバーにしたい
赤い目

BATE FORTE O TAMBOR
QUE EU QUERO
E TIC TIC TIC TAC
МАЛЬЧИК ХОЧЕТ В ТАМБОВ ...

Russian Brazilian Haiku Composed in November in Paris

Swans fly high in the sky
Girls want to go to a bar
Red eyes

Music to listen with it:
Carrapicho, "Tic, Tic Tac."

Utagawa Kuniyoshi, *A Cat Dressed as a Woman Tapping the Head of an Octopus*

Catzilla Attacks!

The giant beast was seen near Mount Fuji in the masterpiece by Hokusai.

If you compare the final version of the masterpiece, restored by Us, to its commonly known sketches at the Library of Congress and at the Rijksmuseum in Amsterdam, you will notice that Our version is much more comprehensible.

Indeed, it is not very believeable that humans would be gazing at birds alone; they are not Cats, to be entertained by flying creatures! But humans love to watch Cats doing weird things endlessly.

Katsushika Hokusai, *Tea House at Koishikawa. The Morning After a Snowfall. Catzilla Attacks.* From *36 Views of Mount Fuji*, no. 11

233

European Art at the End of the Nineteenth and Beginning of the Twentieth Centuries

A New Era Descends the Golden Stairs

What would a new century look like? "Like a Cat coming down a set of golden stairs," thought Edward Burne-Jones at the end of nineteenth century. Thus he foresaw the era of powerful Cats, more than one hundred years before it actually arrived!

This new tendency in Europe brought everything that a Cat can bring: love, warm feelings, happiness, and fun!

Oh, and lots of girls playing music and dancing, of course!

Who are these nice young ladies? Please check the commonly known version of Burne-Jones's masterpiece at the Tate Gallery in London. Maybe you will find the answer there!

Edward Burne-Jones, *The Golden Stairs*

Art or *The Caresses* or *The Sphinx*

We proudly present the result of recent restoration works on the original version of Fernand Khnopff's *Art* (also called *The Sphinx* and *The Caresses*).

The commonly known version of the masterpiece can be found in Belgium, in the Musées Royaux des Beaux-Arts. There the Sphinx has a human head on a Cat's body. This need possessed by art critics of the time, to deny that Cats and humans are equal, is quite astonishing. I mean really, where is the Cat's head?

In this newly restored work, Art presented as a Sphinx finally comes out and recognizes itself as it really is—a Cat!

Fernand Khnopff, *Art* or *The Caresses* or *The Sphinx*

Escaping Criticism

We, Zarathustra the Cat, have already told you how dangerous art critics can be, how their snobbish thinking can inhibit artistic development. It was the subject of the painting *Escaping Criticism* by the famous Catalan artist Pere Borrell del Caso. Though it is not known for certain what the artist intended with the word "criticism" in this title, We're fairly sure it referred to the anti-feline sentiments of the art critics of his day.

If you have a look at the commonly known version of this trompe l'oeil masterpiece, which you can find in the collection of the Bank of Spain, you will see that those irksome critics somehow managed to force the artist to remove Us from his piece. But see how in this original version of the masterpiece We are there in all Our glory declaring, "Exorcise you, art critic! Out! You are banned!"

Pere Borrell del Caso, *Escaping Criticism*

241

A Step to Beauty

The only way to Beauty is through classical ballet. Edgar Degas demonstrated this in so many of his paintings. Here is one of them, whose commonly known version is at the Metropolitan Museum of Art. It shows our first steps in this divine art.

Don't believe those humans who say that you cannot dance if you are fat.

Your grace doesn't depend on your weight.

This young ballet student just received proof of that.

Edgar Degas, *The Dance Class*

The Grace of a Cat

Really, all ballet dancers should be taught by a Fat Cat how to move in the most subtle of ways!

I'm dancing, I'm dancing . . . so am I

. . . and then comes a moment of triumph!

Edgar Degas, *Swaying Dancer (Dancer in Ginger)*

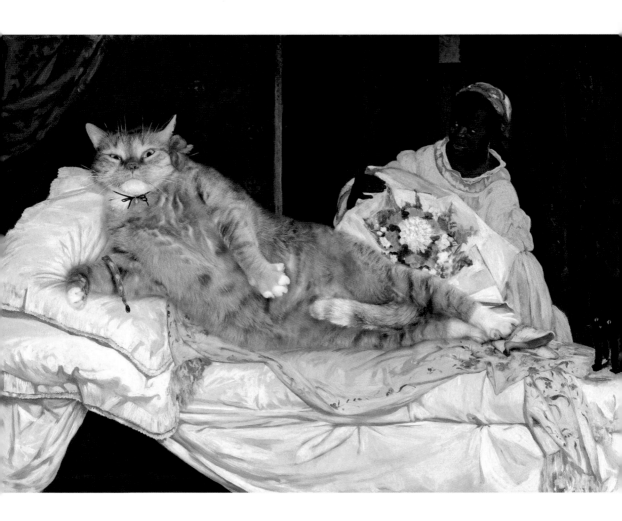

Do Cats Like Flowers?

We are delighted to share with you the true version of Edouard Manet's masterpiece *Olympia*. It is so much more elegant than the commonly known version of the masterpiece at the Musée d'Orsay! There is a subtle tension to this piece that is entirely absent in the revised version. What is it that is missing? The answer: while We do love to adorn ourselves with flowers, flowers do not satisfy Our culinary appetite. For this We Cats actually prefer king prawns or raw meat. To the lady offering Us flowers we say: "Please, take away the flowers and bring Us something We can eat!"

Edouard Manet, *Olympia*, true version

Can I Help You, Sir?

Here We present to you the last version of the world-famous painting of Edouard Manet, *A Bar at the Folies-Bergère*, the last big work by the great master.

In the first and world-renowned version of this masterpiece, which depicts the famous cabaret Folies-Bergère in Paris, one can see the beautiful barmaid Suzon. Having painted her, Edouard Manet realized that a cabaret bar is a bad place for a young lady. Look at her very sad eyes in the first version of the painting at the Musée d'Orsay!

One can find the reason for her sadness in the reflection behind her back: a mustachioed gentleman is asking her to give him something that is definitely not a tangerine. Having in mind this scandalous fact, Manet painted another canvas and placed an honest, brave, orange Cat instead of the poor girl. We were honored to be the model for this painting. We also have a mustache, and We are foolproof.

"Can I help you, Sir?" We ask the mustachioed gentleman. And looking into the honest and sincere Cat's eyes, the gentleman says firmly: "A glass of champagne please, and a couple of tangerines." And keeps his lewd requests to himself!

Edouard Manet, *A Bar at the Folies-Bergère*

The Process of Creation

W hat shall We Cats do when there is nothing to do? We shall involve Ourselves in the process of creation and sit for Claude Monet. The process of creation is very entertaining. Just believe Us.

Claude Monet, *Haystack at Giverny*

Bathing in the Pond of Water Lilies and Other Summer Delights

Summertime. Heat. Cats are melting like clocks in the famous Salvador Dalí painting.

Once Claude Monet saw Us bathing and he was very impressed.

It's so refreshing to plunge into a pond full of water lilies and drink the water tasting of duckweed and flowers!

You can understand how it is by having a closer look at the expression on Our face.

In the background one can see the beginning of the process: We are testing the pond water.

The CAThartic phase of the process is depicted in the latest version of the masterpiece, where We are sitting on the bridge relaxed, contemplating the water lilies.

It's so easy to be lost in space and time during the summer!

If you have a look at the commonly known version of the masterpiece, at the Metropolitan Museum of Art, you will agree that summer is warmer with Cats, isn't it?

And We can reveal a secret: Claude Monet created a life-size portrait of Us in this painting!

Claude Monet, *Bathing in a Pond of Water Lilies*

Do Cats Like Human Kisses?

Our beloved brother and sister Cats, do you like it when your humans kiss you?

Gustav Klimt thought that We love it.

Well, at least, We can tolerate it.

Yes, We can tolerate a lot from Our beloved being, even his weird ways of showing Us affection. A kiss, really what is that? All the civilized world knows that the best way to say "I love you" to a person is:

1. either to make soft head-bumping, forehead to forehead, with somebody you love;

2. or to touch a person's nose with your nose—best if your nose is wet;

3. or, in a very platonic way, to perform a slow eye blink while looking into the eyes of your beloved being.

Gustav Klimt, *The Kiss*, true version

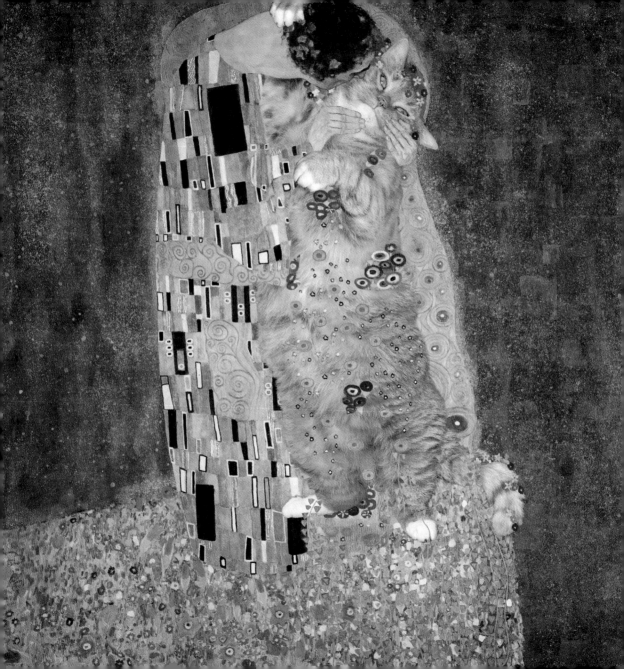

But humans prefer to make this strange movement with their lips on different parts of your precious face. And lucky you are if your human doesn't smoke, drink wine, or eat oranges before this demonstration of his love in such a way!

P.S. It might interest you to know that the great master even went so far as to use a brush made with Our lost whiskers to paint Our fur gold.

Happy End of the World Day!

Have you ever had the feeling that today is the End of the World?
Edvard Munch felt it rather often, and every time he felt it, he painted another version of his thrilling *Scream*.

He needed somebody to support him through this difficult period in his life. So the painter invited Us to pose for another version of his masterpiece.

To persuade us to open Our mouth wide, he gave us a huge spoon of cream.

It was so tasty! *S-cream* became Edvard's masterpiece.

Happy End of the World Da-a-a-a-a-y!

Edvard Munch, *The Scream*

Ready for the Cat

Everything is ready for you—that is the lifestyle of those chosen ones who are named "domestic Cats." With the help of our humans, everything around Us is ready for Our enjoyment. This nice tendency was noticed by Marcel Duchamp, who declared a new kind of art—ready-mades. The most ordinary objects such as a bicycle wheel (or even a urinal) being signed by the artist and put in a new context—a museum, for example—all became pieces of art. The same thing happens when classic masterpieces' images are improved by something good like Cats and mustaches—a new piece of art appears.

In 1919 Marcel Duchamp took a cheap postcard with *Mona Lisa*, drew a mustache and beard on it in pencil, and appended the title *L.H.O.O.Q.* The letters, when pronounced in French, form the sentence "Elle a chaud au cul," which can be translated as "She is hot in the ass." The masculinized female introduces the theme of gender reversal, which was popular with Duchamp.

Nobody knows that he also had a postcard of the true *Mona Lisa*, and also drew a mustache on it. Then he borrowed paper whiskers from Skifcha the Hipster Dubster Cat, world-renowned YouTube star from Moscow, Russia, and glued them onto the

Marcel Duchamp, *L.H.A.O.Q.*

L.H.A.O.Q.
LATSATAK?

Cat's image. He titled the new ready-made *L.H.A.O.Q.*—"Elle a chat au cul." Maybe you can dare to translate it from the French, but not in front of your children! It is very contemporary art, even if it was made a century ago.

This other reversal made his artistic statement stronger. . . .

Having seen this, art critics used to ask Marcel: "Is that art?" And he would always reply, "Yes, yes" in Russian: "Da, da." That is why this art movement is called "dadaism" or simply "dada."

L.H.O.O.Q. was sold for $607,500 on May 13, 1999, at Christie's auction house in New York. We are so kind to think about selling Our *L.H.A.O.Q.* at auction for the Cats' charity. Who will give a better price?

PART XIV

Russian Art at the Beginning of the Twentieth Century

The Rape of Europa

W hat lady would mind being abducted by such a soft, large Cat, as large
as the mythic bull!

Valentin Serov, *The Rape of Europa*

Fat and Skinny

At the beginning of the twentieth century, we were so kind as to let this skinny Russian dancer, Ida Rubenstein, put her famous feet under Our big, soft, warm belly.

Only those of you who have Cats in their houses can imagine what a delight it was for Ida!

Valentin Serov depicted this epic scene.

Valentin Serov, *Ida Rubinstein and the Cat*

Complex Presentiment

You know that Russian art from the beginning of the twentieth century is famous for its abstraction.

What would happen if a Fat Cat and a man from an abstract painting were to meet?

To imagine that, let Us have a look at Kazimir Malevich's painting.

The man and the Cat look at each other.

Both think: "What the . . . ?"

This abstract feeling is called a "complex presentiment."

Now you know the story behind the English title of this work.

Kazimir Malevich, *Complex Presentiment*

Suprematist Cat

But in fact, it appears the Fat Cat and Suprematist Man can become friends once they know each other a little better.

The fact that the Fat Cat is a Suprematist Cat can be ascertained from the fact that his form dominates the painting.

Kazimir Malevich, *Man in Suprematist Landscape with Suprematist Cat*

Manifesto for Cat's Suprematism

We are real. All the artworks in this book are real.
Nobody's opinion about Us, Our art, or this book will ever disturb Our suprematism.

Kazimir Malevich, *Ginger Square* or *Cat's Suprematism*

A Very Solid Cat

After wandering in the labyrinth of suprematic abstractions, We turned into a very solid Cat again.

Ignoramuses may be satisfied by the commonly known version, to be found at the Russian Museum, in which the Cat is not allowed a place at the table. But for anyone who wishes to rest their eyes on the true masterpiece in which Cats and men are seated correctly next to each other . . . Voilà!

Boris Kustodiev, *Cat's Tea with Merchant's Wife*

276

Occupy the Sky

They say: Occupy Wall Street!

We say: Occupy the Sky!

By the way, Russians have the longest known tradition of sky walking.

One can see in the next painting by genius Marc Chagall how people used to promenade over the town of Vitebsk during the years 1914 to 1918.

Marc Chagall, *Over the Town. Occupy the Sky*

Cat Skywalker

Although We never lived in Vitebsk, as Marc Chagall did, We prefer to take our walks this way.

    You, Cats, should try it with Your humans.

Marc Chagall, *The Promenade*

PART XV

European and New World Art of the Twentieth Century and Nowadays

The Persistence of Meowmory

Today, meditating after a delicious repast, We realized that We forgot something very important. We must remember . . . but what? What? What? . . .

Oh, We got it! We should reveal the original version of Dalí's great masterpiece!

Salvador Dalí, *The Persistence of Memory*

The Benefits of Siesta

After a good lunch We have the gracious tendency to appear in the dreams of the great artists.

The sleeping figure of Gala, Dalí's wife and muse, floats above a rock in a tranquil marine landscape. Beside her naked body, two drops of water, a pomegranate, and a bee are also airborne. Gala's dream, prompted by the buzzing of the bee, appears in the upper part of the canvas; there, from an exploding pomegranate shoots out a fish, from whose mouth two playful Cats emerge together with a bayonet, which, one second later, will wake Gala from her restful sleep.

Salvador Dalí, *Dream Caused by the Flight of a Bee Around a Pomegranate a Second Before Waking Up*

Irresistible Temptation

Do you know the worst temptation for a general Cat lover? Of course it is to adopt another Cat!

Do you think Saint Anthony could resist?

Salvador Dalí, *The Temptation of St. Anthony*

FATCATART

Leda and the Cat

Once upon a time in ancient Greece, one Leda couldn't resist the Swan. Nowadays, in the era of atomic energy and the Internet, not one Leda can resist the Cat.

You artists, don't forget: Cats make everything look better, even ladies.

Don't even try to resist the Cat!

Salvador Dalí, *Leda Atomica*

Two Fridas and One Cat

From the story of the Tower of Babel you already know that Cats can unite nations. They can also unite split personalities: it doesn't matter which avatar of Frida is present now, the thing that unites her egos is not only one physical body but also one love for her Cat!

Frida Kahlo, *Two Fridas and One Cat*

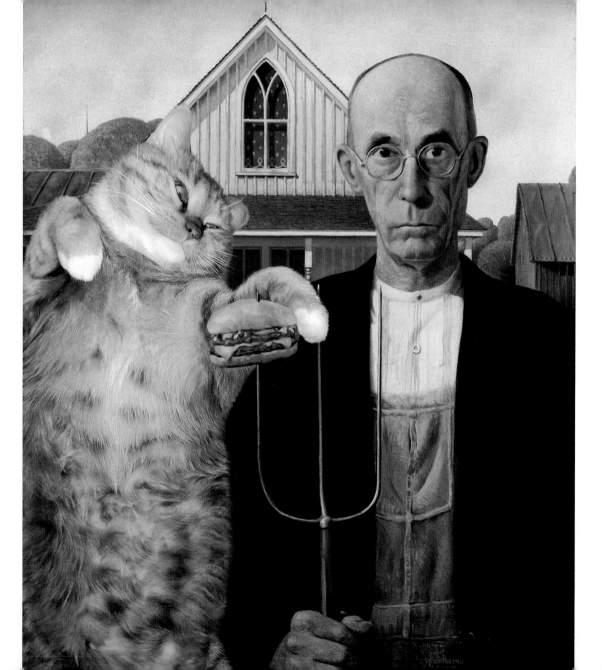

American Gothic Behind Ameri-Cat Politics?

A s you know, We supported Hank the Cat's campaign for Senate.

That is when We realized how horrible human politics are! All those blackmail campaigns that are made against sincere candidates! They said that Hank had never released his birth certificate or his tax returns, and had never responded to allegations of catnip use. Neither is there any record of him serving in any branch of the military!

Why do humans believe these insinuations and even create their own impure fantasies: "Hank is into licking his own genitals! Would you let him date your daughter?"

From the depth of Our heart We tell all humans: We are Cats, We are a Culture, not an LOL. According to the habits of Our race, a person who regularly licks some part of his body demonstrates his purity of thought, self-discipline, and a will for self-improvement.

Sometimes this process of self-perfection gives inspiration to artists, and the traces of that kind of inspiration can be found in masterpieces such as *Haystack in Giverny* by Claude Monet.

They also supposed that We, a Russian Cat, would have nothing to eat in Our

Grant Wood, *American Gothic*. I can has cheezburger?

homeland, so We were seduced by American cheeseburgers. That is why We support Our brother Hank!

Really, humans can be blind! How could We, being a Fat Cat, even performing an obesity management diet, be seduced by a cheeseburger? What nonsense!

Well, yes, really, We are indeed looking at a cheeseburger in *American Gothic* by Grant Wood.

But We swear We are looking at it in a platonic way, contemplating pursuing a doctorate on the theme "Cheeseburger as the Symbol of Vanity and Carnal Temptations in Modern American Culture: From Frank Zappa to Happy Cat." Let them try to digest that!

So don't believe the ignoramuses—they always infuse their impure thoughts into the heads of innocent beings.

Listen to your hearts and vote for Cats!

Thus speaks Zarathustra the Cat.

Giant Octo-Pussy Causes Groundswell

It's a giant octo-pussy that causes the groundswell!

The original version of the famous masterpiece of Edward Hopper.

This painting shows purr-fectly what all the sailors are staring at and why they seem to be hypnotized. Here what is happening is much clearer than in the commonly known version of the masterpiece, which can be found at the Corcoran Gallery of Art in Washington, DC.

Everything makes more sense when a Cat is in the picture, doesn't it?

Edward Hopper, *Groundswell*

Nightcats

If you have ever sat in an empty bar late at night, perhaps you have seen the giant Nightcat passing by.

Edward Hopper, *Nighthawks and Nightcats*

Edward Hopper, *People in the Sun*

People in the Ginger Sun

The true source of sunlight is depicted in this original painting by the great American artist Edward Hopper.

Note that if you compare the original of the famous painting presented here with the commonly known version, which you can find in the Smithsonian American Art Museum, you suddenly realize what Hopper intended with all those huge open spaces: We, the omnipotent feline, are everywhere the eye can see (even if you can't see Us).

Long Way Home

Here We are, the two models for one version of *Christina's World* by Andrew Wyeth.

Do you know that Christina, the subject of this painting, suffered from polio in real life and could no longer walk? This is why she looks to her house as if to some unachievable dream.

So We decided to help her go there. This moment was captured by Andrew Wyeth.

Andrew Wyeth, *Christina's World*

Cats for Presidents!

Our postprandial meditations about the destiny of humanity led us to the inevitable conclusion that only Cats can be perfect governors for humans.

Here is Shepard Fairey's concept art, which is ideal for the first Cat Presidential Candidate.

It is symbolic that the word "KOT3," which means "kitteh" in Russian, has four letters, just as the word "hope" does.

The Cat is the best candidate because Cats never lie; Cats never betray your hopes.

Cats don't steal; the most that a Cat can grab is the sausage on your plate. Cats need food, not money.

The Cat loves you, humans! Humans, love your Cat!

Now you know everything that you need to know about this world and the art in it.

Thus speaks Zarathustra the Cat.

КОТЭ

KITTEH GIVEZ NEW HOPE ★ GREAT ARTISTS' MEWS ★ FATCATART.RU ★ FAMOUS POSTERS IMPROVED BY CATS SINCE 2011

ACKNOWLEDGMENTS

The authors of the book, Svetlana Petrova and Zarathustra the Cat, would like to thank all our friends who helped to create it:

Anthea Norman-Taylor, English and CatSpeak interpreter, longtime friend to Russian artists, host and curator of our first exhibition, and our international agent;

Teresa Longo and Murat Gadeev, Fat Cat Art real-life supporters;

Evgeny Sorokin, Zarathustra the Cat's favorite photographer; Anyona Minina, Zarathustra the Cat's photo sessions partner and caregiver; Alexey Simonenko, Zarathustra the Cat's art consultant; Zarathustra the Cat's PR agents Gareth Davies (UK) and Praskovya Shishkoedova (Russia); Dmitry Masseev, Ksenia Shilovskaya, Irina Besedina, Alexander Schmidt, your help and care were so precious!

Sylvia Krausche, Zarathustra the Cat's assistant in Germany;

Agathe Lichtensztejn, Zarathustra the Cat's art historian;

Sara Carder, Penguin Random House—thank you for finding us!

Jennifer Uram, Penguin Random House—thank you for helping us through the process.

Jane Geerts and Lin Barkass for friendship and support in the UK.

Jana Miloradovskaya and all the friends from Sobaka.ru magazine, who, though its title means "a dog" in Russian, supported Zarathustra the Cat and His humble assistant with the excellent press photos.

Zarathustra the Cat's coworkers in shared projects:

Matthew O'Leary, "Hank for Senate" campaign manager and Hank the Cat, whom we will never forget;

Anna Kondratieva, director of the Cats Museum in St. Petersburg, Russia, and Zarathustra's personal doctor;

Nieto, Claire Pedot, Marilou Chabert (France)—"Catboom!" and "Metacinema" artists, with whom Zarathustra the Cat began his way into cinema.

Friends in art who encouraged development of Fat Cat Art project: Bella Matveeva, Hermes Zygott, Alexande Novikov (Russia); Evan Roth (USA); Max Hattler, Catherine Anyango (UK); Julia Levy (Brazil)—friendly words and deeds meant a lot for us!

Our devoted Facebook friends: Susan Shepard, Terry Genesen Becker, Bridget Norman, Nancy Lucia Lopez, Cat Kingdom, Mitts Gattino, Dave Ross, William Joy, and in fact all others social media fans—your feedback is so important!

Rijksmuseum Amsterdam, which shared professional .tff scans of paintings in their collection and created a Rijksstudio where everybody can download pictures in high res and create their own art based on them; SMK, National Gallery of Denmark; Metropolitan Museum of Art in New York; National Gallery in Washington, DC; Library of Congress in Washington, DC; the J. Paul Getty Museum in Los Angeles; and all other museums that support sharing their public domain art.

The Russian Museum and the Hermitage Museum for inspiring us in St. Petersburg.

If you enjoyed this book, visit

www.tarcherbooks.com

and sign up for Tarcher's e-newsletter to receive
special offers, giveaway promotions, and
information on hot upcoming releases.

TARCHER
PENGUIN

Great Lives Begin with Great Ideas

Connect with the Tarcher Community

• • •

Stay in touch with favorite authors!
Enter weekly contests!
Read exclusive excerpts!
Voice your opinions!

Follow us

 Tarcher Books

 @TarcherBooks

If you would like to place a bulk order
of this book, call 1-800-847-5515.